**East**

David A Hayes

ISBN 0 904491 40 4

*Mecklenburgh Square, east side, 1967*

# *East of* Bloomsbury

Compiled by   David A Hayes

Edited by   F Peter Woodford

Designed by   Ivor Kamlish

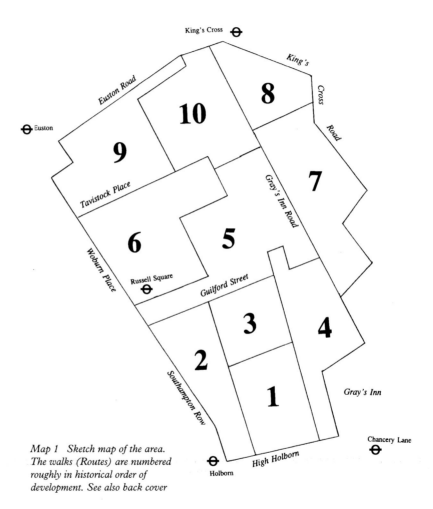

King's Cross

Euston Road

Euston

King's

Cross

Road

10

8

9

Tavistock Place

7

Woburn Place

6

5

Gray's Inn Road

Russell Square

Guilford Street

3

4

2

1

Southampton Row

Gray's Inn

High Holborn

Chancery Lane

Holborn

*Map 1  Sketch map of the area.
The walks (Routes) are numbered
roughly in historical order of
development. See also back cover*

# Contents

# Acknowledgements

The research and text were almost entirely the work of David Hayes, but the following members of the Camden History Society Research Team all made insightful corrections and cogent suggestions:

Sheila Ayres, Roger Cline, Liz Eccleshare, Ruth Hayes, David Hellings, Michael Ogden, Sue Palmer, Tatiana Wolff

Special thanks are due to David Hellings for his painstaking, footslogging work following the directions to readers in the first draft, clarifying them where necessary, checking the current look of every building (they change with bewildering frequency!), and adding pungent architectural comments.

Most of the illustrations were provided with the aid of the unfailingly knowledgeable Borough Archivist Malcolm Holmes and the staff of the Camden Local Studies and Archive Centre, led by Richard Knight, who acted with their usual efficiency and courtesy. The following also provided and gave permission to reproduce illustrations: the National Monuments Record (frontispiece), London Metropolitan Archives (Figs 4, 8 and 12), the Working Men's College (Fig 5) and the author (Fig 11). The sketch map by Ivor Kamlish was based on Ordnance Survey maps of 1914, adapted to reflect subsequent change.

## A note on typeface codes

Buildings named or numbered in the text in **bold** type were extant and visible at the time of writing (January 1998); those in roman type had either been demolished or had otherwise faded into the past.

# Illustrations

# Historical Overview

Almost all the area with which this book is concerned was once monastic land. By 1405 the monks of the London Charterhouse had come into possession of two adjoining medieval manors: **Blemundsbury** (or Bloomsbury), largely in the parish of St Giles-in-the-Fields, a narrow strip whose territory lies along our western boundary; and, to the north-east, the **Lay Manor of St Pancras**, one of several manors in a large parish extending some 4 miles northwards to Highgate. Nearer the City, and mostly in Holborn parish, was **Portpool** manor, property of the Priory of St Bartholomew, West Smithfield. By 1370 its manorhouse had become a 'hospitium' for lawyers, the beginnings of Gray's Inn. At the Dissolution of the Monasteries (1536-40), their property was confiscated by the Crown and disposed of in various ways. Bloomsbury passed to the Earls of Southampton (and later, through marriage, to the Dukes of Bedford), while land ownership elsewhere in our area became very fragmented.

By the later 17th century, London's built-up area had crept north from the Thames to reach medieval Gray's Inn and the main road from the City westward now known as High Holborn. North of this, apart from a few isolated buildings, all was meadow land, where dairy cattle grazed and city folk enjoyed such pleasurable pursuits as country walks, watercress gathering, or wildfowling on the many small ponds which dotted the area — but it was a district dangerous after dark, reputedly a haunt of highwaymen and cut-throats.

The main route to the north here was Gray's Inn Lane, which at Battle Bridge (now King's Cross) crossed the river **Fleet**, the eastern boundary of the parish of St Pancras. Also known as the River of Wells, it was bordered by several 18th-century spas, two of which lay within our survey area. The locality was renowned for the purity of both its air and its water. A small tributary of the river Fleet bisected the area, running south of the line of Guilford Street before veering south-east along the course of Roger Street. This, together with various springs, served as a source for two conduits built to carry water to the City, one medieval, the other Elizabethan. The later of these lent its name to **Lamb's Conduit Fields**, a term loosely applied to the meadows stretching northwards towards the line of the present Euston Road. Reminders of both conduits will be encountered on our walks. By contrast, no trace remains of the earthworks thrown up across the local fields during the Civil War, part of the fortifications built around London to guard against a Royalist attack. They ran to the north of the **King's Way**, a royal field road (the line of present Theobalds Road), used by the Stuart kings to reach Hertfordshire and beyond.

Urbanisation of the area was slow and piecemeal, spanning over 150 years. Plague and Fire (1665-6) forced many prosperous Londoners out of the City to live on its fringes: many gained a taste for suburban living and never returned. By the mid-1680s houses for merchants and professionals had been built at the west end of what we know as Theobalds Road. Two decades earlier, and a little further west, the Earl of Southampton, lord of Bloomsbury manor, had laid out the capital's first square (now Bloomsbury Square), a move soon to be emulated inside our area by the speculative builder Nicholas Barbon. In 1684 he developed Red Lion Square, before turning his attention to two neighbouring estates - both, coincidentally, charitable endowments: the **Bedford Charity** (or **Harpur**) estate, straddling Theobalds Road; and, to its north, astride Lamb's Conduit Street, the **Rugby** school estate (see Map 2).

By 1720, palatial Powis House had arisen off (Great) Ormond Street, and noble Queen Square was being laid out to the west on a strip of land bordering the

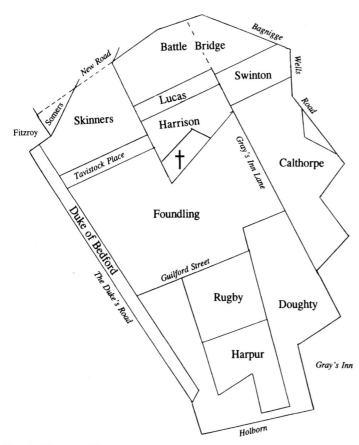

Map 2 Diagram of the major
estates underlying the area.

Bedford estate, intended to attract a more aristocratic class of resident. St George the Martyr church, built as a chapel of ease for the new residential district, achieved parochial status in 1723, its small rectangular parish carved out of one corner of St Andrew Holborn (Map 3, p 11). Eight years later St Giles, to the west, was similarly divided: the resulting new parish of St George's Bloomsbury had an irregular boundary projecting north-eastward into our area as far as its former burial ground (now St George's Gardens).

For the next 70 years the line of Guilford Street marked the northern edge of the built-up area. In 1745, new premises for the **Foundling Hospital** (FH) were built on a 56-acre field to the north. This remarkable institution occupied the site of Coram's Fields, the meadows on either side remaining undeveloped: Queen Square residents could still enjoy rural views northward. (Map 6, p 96) Lending renewed impetus to the development of the area was the opening in the late 1750s of London's first by-pass, a turnpike intended to ease troop movements and allow cattle to be driven to the City markets while avoiding the congested streets of Holborn and St Giles. It was known as the **New Road** from Paddington to Islington until 1857, when the Camden section was renamed Euston Road after the Suffolk country seat of the Duke of Grafton, whose land it crossed. Ribbon development along the New Road began in the 1790s: Somers Town, built at that time to the north (and just outside our area) was, for a decade or more, indeed a distinct 'town', separated from the capital by many acres of farm land. The northward march of the metropolis had, however, already resumed. By 1790 a cash-strapped FH had decided to lease its spare land for house-building, resulting in the twin squares of Brunswick and Mecklenburgh, and a grid of less elegant streets nearby, in whose development the builder James Burton was a major player. An eastward extension of Guilford Street across the **Doughty** estate spurred Henry Doughty to complete the development of his property begun decades earlier by his forebears.

Infill from Tavistock Place to the New Road was under way by c1807, when Burton leased land on the **Skinners'** estate, which stretched from Burton Street to Tonbridge Street, and was vested in the Skinners' Company as trustees for Tonbridge School (Kent). To the east was the small **Lucas** estate, on which Cromer Street had been begun in 1801. To its south, Regent Square was laid out in 1822 on land owned by the brickmaking **Harrison** family. Immediately south of King's Cross, and the last part of our area to be developed (1824-40), was the portion of the **Battle Bridge** estate round Argyle Square, where house building was completed only after the demise of the over-ambitious Panarmonion project (p 79).

Meanwhile, south-east of Battle Bridge, building had begun as early as 1767, encouraged by the advent of the New Road, and resulting in a little Georgian suburb centred on Britannia Street. To the south, the land sloped steeply down from Gray's Inn Lane to the banks of Fleet. Here, east of the Lane, was the estate of Lord **Calthorpe**, part of old Portpool manor, which underwent a mixture of residential and industrial development from about 1810, the predominant builder here being Thomas Cubitt.

Our area was at first almost wholly residential. Lying on the Bloomsbury borders, it has long attracted artists, writers and intellectuals of all kinds, often while young and making their way in the world, though some settled (and died) locally after finding fame or fortune. The 19th century saw the transformation of the area into the very mixed one it is today. Various light industries colonised streets near the main roads and the valley of the Fleet. Printing and metalworking were among the district's staple industries, as were the making of scientific instruments and plaster figures, both occupations associated with the Italian community. Italians arrived in London in two phases — political exiles, usually middle-class, at the time of the Napoleonic Wars, followed later in the century by poor economic migrants from the depressed Italian countryside. Poverty and affluence coexisted cheek by jowl. By 1850 many of the mews areas and lesser streets had declined into slums, some to be replaced later by model dwellings for the 'deserving poor', or 'chambers' and 'mansion' flats for the rather better-heeled.

The railway revolution brought three main lines south to termini on Euston Road, encouraging a proliferation of hotels, both large and small, in several parts of our area. Many houses became offices, lawyers in particular favouring the streets near Gray's Inn, while trade unions were attracted to the area south of King's Cross. Numerous charities (many devoted to the welfare of women or children) established headquarters locally, in an area which had at its centre, in the Foundling Hospital, the world's first charitable corporation — a locality which Robert Louis Stevenson once described as 'made for the humanities and the alleviation of all hard destinies'. Yet more houses were taken over by institutions, medical, educational or religious, and some were later demolished to make way for purpose-built premises, the cluster of hospitals in and near Queen Square being a good example.

In the Second World War (WW II) few parts of the district were wholly unscathed, as is suggested by the large number of buildings under 50 years old. Three thousand bombs, largely incendiaries, fell on Holborn, taking 426 lives and

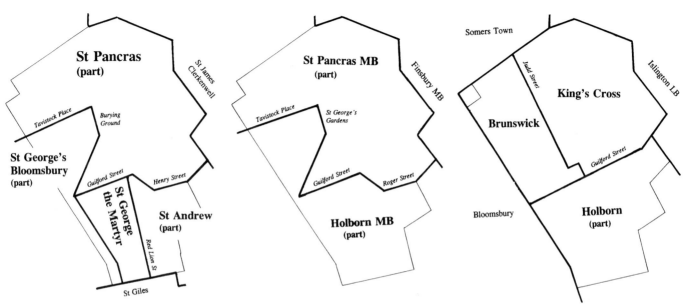

*Map 3  Parishes before 1900.*

*Map 4  Metropolitan Boroughs, 1900-1964.*

*Map 5  Wards of the London Borough of Camden, 1998.*

destroying a seventh of the borough's buildings. Among the areas worst affected was the western end of Theobalds Road, where devastation was total: further north the neighbourhood south of King's Cross was also badly hit. The areas of greatest destruction underwent major redevelopment, with social housing in some places, office blocks in others. The University of London continued its

expansion eastward into the area, which includes several of its institutes and student halls of residence. Those streets which survived WW II were in a sorry state, through damage or neglect: 'grimy' and 'sordid' typify the language used by writers after the war to describe what are now some of the capital's most agreeable streets. In 1998 it is pleasing to witness the effects of two decades of restoration,

regeneration and gentrification, and to note a trend towards conversion back to residential use of many houses that were made into offices over a century ago.


The administrative changes, from parish vestries to Metropolitan Boroughs to electoral wards of the London Borough of Camden are shown in maps 3-5 above.

11

# Streets in the area
**renamed in the course of time**

(those in italics were renamed before 1901)

| Present name | Earlier name(s) |
|---|---|
| AMPTON PLACE | Frederick Place |
| ARGYLE STREET | |
| *S arm* | Manchester Street |
| ARGYLE WALK | *Argyle Place + North Place* |
| BEDFORD ROW | *Bedford Walk* |
| BELGROVE STREET | Belgrave Street |
| BIDBOROUGH ST | |
| *E end* | *Claremont Place* |
| BIRKENHEAD ST | Liverpool Street |
| BOSWELL STREET | Devonshire Street |
| BURTON PLACE | Crescent Place |
| CALTHORPE STREET | |
| *E end* | *Calthorpe Terrace* |
| *middle* | *Lower Calthorpe Street* |
| CARTWRIGHT GDNS | Burton Crescent |
| COLEY STREET | Wilson Street |
| COLONNADE | *Colonnade Mews* |
| CORAM STREET | Great Coram Street |
| COSMO PLACE | *Fox Ct + Little Ormond St* |
| CRESTFIELD ST | Chesterfield Street |
| CROMER STREET | |
| *W end* | *Greenland Place* |
| *rest* | *Lucas Street* |
| CUBITT STREET | *Arthur Street* |
| DANE STREET | Leigh Street |
| DOMBEY STREET | East Street |
| DOUGHTY STREET | *Upper John Street* |
| DUKE'S ROAD | Woburn Buildings |

| Present name | Earlier name(s) |
|---|---|
| EMERALD STREET | *Green Street* |
| EUSTON ROAD | *The New Road; various Terraces & Places* |
| FLAXMAN TERRACE | *Draper's Place; Brantome Place* |
| GAGE STREET | *Cross Street* |
| GRAY'S INN ROAD | *Portpoole Lane; Gray's Inn Lane; various Terraces & Places* |
| GREAT ORMOND ST | |
| *E end* | *New Ormond Street* |
| *W end* | *Ormond Street* |
| GUILFORD PLACE | *Lamb's Conduit Place* |
| HANDEL STREET | *Henrietta Street* |
| HASTINGS STREET | *Speldhurst Street* |
| HERBRAND STREET | |
| *N end* | *Little Coram Street* |
| *middle* | *Little Guilford Street* |
| *S end* | *Colonnade* |
| JOCKEY'S FIELDS | *Bedford Mews* |
| JUDD STREET | |
| *S end* | *Hunter Street North* |
| KENTON STREET | |
| *S end* | *Wilmott Street* |
| KING'S CROSS RD | *Bagnigge Wells Road* |
| LAMB'S CONDUIT | |
| PASSAGE | *Little Conduit Street* |
| STREET | *Red Lion Street (pt)* |
| LEEKE STREET | *Charlotte Street* |
| LOXHAM STREET | *Riley Street* |
| MARCHMONT ST | |
| *S end* | *Everett Street* |

| Present name | Earlier name(s) |
|---|---|
| MECKLENBURGH PL. | Caroline Place |
| MIDHOPE STREET | *Wood Street* |
| NORTHINGTON ST | Little James Street |
| OLD GLOUCESTER ST | Gloucester Street |
| PRINCETON STREET | *Prince's Street* |
| QUEEN SQUARE | Devonshire Square |
| ROGER STREET | Henry Street |
| RUGBY STREET | Chapel Street |
| ST CHAD'S PLACE | |
| *E end* | *Fifteen Foot Lane* |
| ST CHAD'S STREET | Derby Street |
| SANDLAND STREET | *Bedford Street* |
| SANDWICH STREET | *Hadlow Street* |
| SEAFORD STREET | *Francis Street* |
| SWINTON PLACE | Cross Street |
| TANKERTON STREET | *Dutton Street* |
| TAVISTOCK PLACE | |
| *E end* | *Cox Street; Compton Street* |
| THANET STREET | *Lancaster Street* |
| THEOBALDS ROAD | |
| *W end* | *Theobalds Row* |
| *E end* | *King's Way; King's Road* |
| TONBRIDGE STREET | |
| *S end* | *Brunswick Street* |
| *N end* | *Joseph Street* |
| WHIDBORNE STREET | *Brighton Street* |
| WICKLOW STREET | |
| *S end* | *George Street* |
| *middle* | *Little George Street* |
| *N end* | *Paradise Street* |
| WREN STREET | Wells Street |

## Route 1
# Red Lion Square and the Harpur Estate

*(see back cover for map)*

**B**egin this circular walk from Holborn Underground station by walking eastwards along High Holborn and, crossing at the next set of lights, turn left along the east side of **PROCTER STREET**. Created in 1961-62 as part of a new one-way traffic system, this is both lined and spanned by contemporary **Procter House**, largely unoccupied after 35 years, and about (1998) to be refurbished.

Ignoring Eagle Street take the second right, out of the district's newest street and into one of London's oldest squares. It was in **RED LION SQUARE** that development of our area began in 1684. Dr Nicholas Barbon, an unscrupulous surgeon turned speculative builder, not content with the destruction of several of the great houses along the Strand, now set about developing a 17-acre greenfield site in Red Lion Fields. His initiative provoked a violent response from the gentlemen of neighbouring Gray's Inn. Incensed at the loss of their rural views, 100 of them descended on the site, and a pitched battle ensued between them and Barbon's workmen, with bricks as missiles. Unabashed, and defying legal bids to stop

him, the 'doctor' proceeded with the building of the square. Seven short streets or passageways radiated from its corners and sides; a short-lived obelisk in the centre of the gardens once commemorated Oliver Cromwell and his fellow regicides Ireton and Bradshaw. Tradition has it that their bodies were brought to rest in nearby Red Lion Yard (off High Holborn) after being disinterred from Westminster Abbey, and before being dragged through the streets to Tyburn for public exposure on a gibbet.

Watch-houses, demolished by Act of Parliament in 1737, stood at each corner of the square. Early opinions on the square (Fig 1, p14) differed: 'a pleasant square of good buildings between Holborn south and the fields north', wrote one observer; 'the most desolate square in London', complained another. The Earl of Hardwick lived here in 1725-31; John Wilkes, Lord Mayor of London, in 1774. Five years earlier a Dr Armstrong had founded here London's first dispensary for the relief of the 'infant poor'.

---

### Street names along route 1 and their origin

| | |
|---|---|
| **Bedford** | **Lamb's Conduit** |
| Local land endows charities in the town of Bedford | Water supply to the City, financed by William Lambe |
| **Dane** | **North** |
| A St Clement Danes parish charity owns land locally | North of Red Lion Square |
| **Dombey** | **Princeton** |
| Dickens' *Dombey and Son* | Variant on earlier Prince's |
| **Drake** | **Procter** |
| Unknown | The poet Bryan Waller Procter (Barry Cornwall) lived in Red Lion Square |
| **Eagle** | **Red Lion** |
| Tavern and brewhouse, demolished 1793 | Old tavern in High Holborn |
| **Emerald** | **Richbell** |
| From earlier Green (see p 18) | Local speculative builder |
| **Harpur** | **Sandland** |
| Sir William Harpur (or Harper), benefactor of the Bedford Charity | Unknown |
| | **Theobalds** |
| | Hertfordshire hunting park of the Stuart kings |

We start an anticlockwise circuit of the square on the south side, where Procter House North has supplanted former No.10, for over a century home to the Royal College of Veterinary Surgeons (now removed to Mayfair). A blue plaque on the side wall of post-WW II **Summit House** recalls the residence on the site, 1752-76, of John Harrison, whose perfection of the marine chronometer was eventually (1773) recognised as providing the most accurate way of determining longitude at sea. The site was later occupied by St Paul's Hospital for Skin and Genito-Urinary Diseases. Arnold Bennett stayed at a

friend's flat in Victorian **Halsey House** in 1902, the year in which *Anna of the Five Towns* appeared. Although the square suffered grave damage in 1941, some 18th-century houses survive on the south-east side.

Re-fronted **No.17** was home in 1851 to the painter Dante Gabriel Rossetti, required by his landlord to keep his models 'under some gentlemanly restraint, as some artists sacrifice the dignity of art to the baseness of passion'. The same house in 1856-9 was shared by the painter Edward Burne-Jones and the wide-ranging William Morris, cared for by a housekeeper nicknamed 'Red Lion Mary'. An LCC signboard recalls the residence of all three artists. In 1861 the celebrated firm of Morris, Marshall, Faulkner & Co. was founded at No.8 (again on the site of Procter House North), with a kiln in the basement for firing tiles and stained glass.

**Brampton** flats stand in the south-east corner of the square, where Red Lion Passage, a preserve of publishers, once ran off diagonally, just as Lamb's Conduit Passage still does from the north-east corner. **Tresham** flats occupy the site of the office of the Sheriffs of Middlesex, and of No. 23, where the much-travelled Jonas Hanway died in 1798. A benefactor of the Foundling Hospital, he is also remembered

*1    18th-century Red Lion Square, looking north towards (Great) Ormond Street.*

as the first man to carry an umbrella.

On the north side of the square, **Conway Hall** (1929) is home to the South Place Ethical Society (named after its original location in Finsbury). Founded in 1839 by Moncure Conway, a liberal Christian, it became agnostic 30 years later, but its winter programme of Sunday chamber music concerts, which began in 1887, continues a long tradition of permissible sabbath-day activity. An anti-fascist demonstration outside the hall in 1974 turned into the notorious Red Lion Square Riot, the death in which of Warwick student Kevin Gately prompted an inquiry by Lord Scarman.

Rose-tinted **New Mercury House** (Cable & Wireless; see also its parent Mercury House, p 17) stands on a site occupied at various times by a Jewish school, the Trinitarian Bible Society, the British Asylum for Deaf & Dumb Females, the Home for Penitent Women, and the University Tutorial College, where H G Wells once taught. No.28 was home in 1928 to actress Fay Compton. No.31 in 1854 saw the foundation by F D Maurice of the Working Men's College, soon to move to Great Ormond Street (p 28). **Churchill House** at No.35 was once home to the publishers Cassell's. Sir Winston, one of their authors, laid the foundation stone. The firm relocated to Westminster in the early 1980s, taking with them a reclining statue of the native-

American princess Pocahontas, which had long been a feature of the square. In compensation we now have, at the east end of the gardens, a bust by Marcelle Quinton of the philosopher Bertrand Russell, who lectured at Conway Hall. It was unveiled by Mrs Dora Russell in 1980. At the opposite end is a small 1985 statue of the pacifist Fenner Brockway, reinstated after damage in the Great Storm of 1987.

Long-lost No.1, on the west side of the square (across what is now Procter Street), was the London Dispensary for Diseased and Ulcerated Legs, founded in 1857 under the auspices of Florence Nightingale. In the following year No.4 witnessed an early demonstration of refrigeration by engineer James Harrison. St John the Evangelist (Fig 2, p 16), a beautiful 1000-seat church by J L Pearson, once dominated this side of the square, from its consecration in 1878 to its destruction in 1941, after which its ruins faced what had by then become the Bloomsbury trolleybus terminus. On the site today is the large 1961 block of Westminster University's School of Law, formerly part of the Polytechnic of Central London, and earlier the LCC's Holborn College of Law, Language & Commerce, itself a merger of two institutions, of which Princeton College (p 19) was one.

Stay on the east side of Procter Street, and turn north along its continuation, **DRAKE STREET**. All of 40 paces long,

it was already bereft of its original 12
houses by Edwardian times. It was much
widened as part of the 1960s' one-way
system. Veering right, use the zebra
crossing to reach the north side of
**THEOBALDS ROAD**. Often
pronounced 'Tibbalds Road' by local
people ('Tybalds Close' is the name coined
by Camden Council for its neighbouring
housing estate), this once formed part of
the King's Way, a private field road used
by the Stuart kings to reach both
Newmarket and their hunting park at
Theobalds (Herts.). By the early 18th
century houses had been built at this
western end, then known as Theobalds
Row. The antiquarian John le Neve was
living here in 1717 when his *Monumenta
Anglicana* was published. In 1878, the
carriageway was widened and the Row was
integrated with its eastern continuation,
until then still known as King's Road.
Tramlines were laid down here by the
North Metropolitan, a company operating
mainly in East London. Until 1905-6 its
horse-drawn cars ran from Clerkenwell and
points east to a terminus at the west end
of Theobalds Road. The tramway was
then electrified and extended into the new
Kingsway tunnel (the only central link
between tramways north and south of the

*2    Interior view of St John the Evangelist
Church, Pearson's masterpiece, destroyed in
1941.*

river), with power supplied through a conduit laid under the roadway. A new direct road link with Vernon Place and Bloomsbury Way turned Theobalds Road into the major traffic route it is today.

All but flattened in WW II, its north side hereabouts is now wholly modern, lined by post-war office blocks of 9-10 storeys. At **No.124** is stone-faced **Mercury House** (1955, refurbished 1992), headquarters of Cable & Wireless, adorned by reliefs depicting the airborne messenger of the gods. Set in the protruding wall to the left of the main door, at pavement level, is a tiny inscription marking the historic boundary of the Bedford Charity estate, which once bisected the block. Sir William Harpur (or Harper), a Lord Mayor of London who died in 1573, left 13 acres and one rood of meadow land in 'Conduit Shott' to provide dowries for girls in his native town of Bedford, and to endow a grammar school which he had recently re-founded there.

After a rationalisation of boundaries with a neighbouring landowner in 1654, the Bedford Charity (or Harpur) estate comprised an L-shaped area running east from Mercury House to Emerald Street, then crossing Theobalds Road and embracing land between Bedford Row and Red Lion Street. By 1684 the charity trustees were in negotiation with Barbon, anxious to maximise revenue, but suspicious of the shifty, near-bankrupt

'doctor'. A complex legal wrangle was still unresolved when he proceeded to erect houses willy-nilly on both the Harpur and neighbouring Rugby estates. It is not clear how much of the area was completed by Barbon, although the street plan was certainly his; he died in 1698, ruined by a national financial crisis, leaving houses half finished. A contemporary account compared one uncompleted street to the 'ruins of Troy'.

Mercury House stands on the site of the Harpur Arms, which until c.1913 had boasted a galleried yard of the kind now seen in London only at the George in Southwark. Next door was a luxurious picture-house, one of the first in Britain with an American-style soda fountain. Opened in 1922 as the Bloomsbury Victory cinema, and later renamed the Bloomsbury Super, it evolved into a news theatre before suffering a direct hit in WW II. Eastward stand two large red-brick office blocks thrown up by the Government in 1948-50, and condemned by Nikolaus Pevsner as 'crushingly utilitarian'. Ariel House, for the Ministry of Civil Aviation, later became **Adastral House** of the Air Ministry, its new name coined from the motto of the RAF; while **Lacon House**, built around three sides of a courtyard, was originally occupied by the Board of Trade. Both blocks were in use by the MOD until its mass exodus to Bristol c.1996. Among the buildings they replaced were the White

Horse pub at No.98 and the Cross Keys at No.80, a music hall of some note in 1867-87, which vied with another (the Lord Raglan) almost exactly opposite.

Look across to the south side of Theobalds Road, where some Victorian buildings escaped destruction in WW II, and where Bradlaugh House at **No.47** is headquarters of the British Humanist Association, the National Secular Society, and the South Place Ethical Society, proprietors of the adjoining Conway Hall. Modern blocks to the right cover the site of former No.15, birthplace in 1875 of Samuel Coleridge-Taylor, composer of *Hiawatha*.

**OLD NORTH STREET**, the northern egress from Red Lion Square, is continued by **NEW NORTH STREET**, into which we turn. In 1753, before the introduction of house numbering, a hatter was recorded as living here at, paradoxically, the sign of the 'Golden Leg'. Nothing remains of Barbon's houses, and the later tenements of Dunstable Court have given way to the post-WW II council flats of **Springwater**, a name recalling the district's aqueous associations. The street's Victorian northern end includes a public house, known for generations as the George & Dragon until renamed the Moon c.1980. It has since become **Murphy's Moon**, the first of several 1990s Irish 'theme pubs' we shall encounter. Opposite is a former printing works, later occupied by makers of fencing swords, and now refurbished as offices labelled 'Leon Paul'.

Here turn eastward along what was once the western end of Dombey Street, taking care not to trip on an unexpected 'sleeping policeman'. Originally part of Barbon's East Street, this is now a footway flanked by the flats and gardens of 6-storey **Windmill** and 10-storey **Blemundsbury**, designed by Hening & Chitty, and completed 1949. Pevsner (a year later) was strangely complimentary about these blocks: 'not lavish, but of delicate precision and agreeably devoid of mannerisms ... [with] prettily detailed balconies'. Although Blemundsbury (as Bloomsbury was once known) is a laudable attempt at a historically relevant name, we are here some way to the east of that medieval manor! The block covers the site of No.30 Dombey Street, in whose garden lay one of the sources of Lamb's Conduit (p 32).

Beyond, intersecting from the right, and separating the two government-built blocks we have already met in Theobalds Road, is **HARPUR STREET**. Dr John Fothergill, a Quaker specialising in sore throats, died here in 1780. The surviving **No.10** at the north end of the street has a fine Doric portico with a broken pediment, and dates from 20 years earlier. **Bevan John House** next door looks as old, but was purpose-built as flats, and must date from a rebuilding of the street c.1883. In the rebuilt Harpur Street, Nos.7-9 were an early headquarters of the Society for the Prevention of Cruelty to Children (now NSPCC), which ran a rescue home here for badly treated youngsters. An archway burrows through Bevan John House into private **Harpur Mews**, once the yard of James Soanes, whose Victorian business here combined stationery supply with waste paper disposal.

**DOMBEY STREET**, which now runs only east of Harpur Street, was renamed in 1936 after Dickens' *Dombey and Son*, but although the author lived for a while in nearby Doughty Street (p 39), the novel has no particular local associations. In this still wholly residential street, **Nos.9-15** form a uniform row of handsome 4-storey houses of the early 18th century (re-fronted 1765-7), with unusually slender pedimented doorways, and basements approached by very narrow steps, all sensitively restored by the Circle 33 Housing Trust. The dignified range opposite at **Nos.18-22** was much altered in the 19th century. Set in the walls of No.22 and of its neighbour (No.2 Orde Hall Street) are boundary plaques inscribed *BCB 1883* (for Bedford Charity Bounds) and *Rugby Estate 1884*.

On reaching **LAMB'S CONDUIT STREET**, pause to look to the right (southward). Begun by Barbon in the 1680s, the street was for 90 years regarded as an extension of Red Lion Street (p 19). Although most of it (p 32) lies on Rugby land, its once war-torn southern end was on the Harpur estate. The 1930s blue-tiled building on this corner at **No.27**, on the site of a former bicycle factory, was occupied first by a firm of house furnishers, and later by Longmans the publishers. Of the many charities with headquarters locally, none was so intriguingly named as the Society for the Prevention of Premature Burial, which c.1900 occupied a house on the Lacon House site. At **No.10**, a 13-storey office development of the Harpur Trust, is the Aliens' Registration Office. An earlier foreign presence on the site, at No.15, was the business of the French Pathé brothers, later of newsreel fame, but described in 1906 as phonograph makers. The modern flats of **Rapier House** cover the site of No.40, where the Bloomsbury Synagogue stood for many years until the 1960s.

Turn left along Lamb's Conduit Street (*for this stretch see p 32*) and then right along an alleyway forming one arm of L-shaped **EMERALD STREET**. This was originally Green Street, possibly after either Edmond Greene, the first headmaster of Bedford School, or a bowling green associated with a nearby cockpit (p 37). On the left, above the rear entrance to the former French's Dairy (p 33), two stones (dated 1776 and 1838) mark the Rugby/Harpur boundary. Exchanges of property between the two estates meant that the street has belonged at different times to both. Turning right, notice a further plaque, set in the wall of **Nos.26-34**, an old printing and bookbinding works: 'Bedford Bounds', it declares, referring, of course, to the Bedford Charity (Harpur) estate rather than the better-known ducal demesne to the west. The north-south section of the street is lined by 4-storey factories and warehouses, products of the 19th-century commercialisation of the area. Old taking-in doors survive in abundance, such as those at **Nos.20-24**, once a sponge warehouse, and at **Nos.11-15** and **Nos.23-29**, both former printing works. Printing has been replaced as the street's staple industry by the modern sister profession of graphic design. Little **RICHBELL PLACE**, leading off to the right, was built as a cul-de-sac in 1710 by one John Richbell.

We re-emerge into **THEOBALDS ROAD**, alongside the **Queen's Head** pub, whose inscriptions testify to its establishment in 1812 and rebuilding 65 years later. Turn right along Theobalds Road, which here is lined by rather grim buildings of 1878-80, with shops and cafés at street level, some of them helpfully sporting their dates of construction and owners' initials: for instance, the letters 'FK' on several buildings must refer to Frederick Kingwell, a prominent local landlord in the late 19th century. Maybe it was to such a man that a young H G Wells

paid his 4 shillings a week when in 1888 he rented an unidentified attic room in Theobalds Road, with paper-thin walls which rendered conversation impossible when traffic was going by.

Passing the modern Holborn **police station**, cross at the traffic lights to the south side of the road, noting on the corner, at **No.25**, a sign for the brass foundry of Messrs Yannedis, a long-established, lately departed, firm of architectural ironmongers. Behind, and running diagonally through to Red Lion Square, is **LAMB'S CONDUIT PASSAGE**, once noted for its small jobbing printers, some of whose shop fronts remain.

**RED LION STREET**, along which we turn southward, dates from the late 17th century, and was originally residential, attracting professional people, notably solicitors. It later evolved into a Victorian 'high street' of shops and eating places. After heavy wartime damage, it is now an untidy mix of old and new, including some uninspired modern office blocks built by the Harpur Trust. A **Dolphin** tavern 'in Red Lion fealds' was recorded as early as 1690. Its Victorian successor at the north end of the street was half destroyed in a 1915 Zeppelin raid. Opposite at No.38 is the luckier **Enterprise** (its sign a sailing ship), a 19th-century rebuild of an earlier 'Grapes'. An Italian restaurant occupies **No.46**, one of a dozen surviving, though

much altered, early houses, while the Mazzini-Garibaldi Club, founded as a facility for working men in 1861, is at **No.51** - reminders that the district was a hub of London's Italian community before its centre of gravity drifted eastward to Saffron Hill. Red Lion Street was once noted for its *figurini* and sellers of plaster casts.

Turn left along **PRINCETON STREET**. On the south side is the former Prince's Street Board School of 1877, but entered through a curiously classical archway. The building served after WW II as the LCC's Princeton College of Language of Commerce, and is now the **Holborn Centre for the Performing Arts**, part of Kingsway College. Opposite stands a modern block housing the Inns of Court School of Law, with a car park in what was once Dog & Duck Yard. Turn right at Bedford Row, the eastern boundary of the Harpur estate. Although most of the west side belongs to the Bedford Charity, and its estate office was once at No.26, much of the Row belonged to the Doughty family and their forebears, and we shall return to it later (p 35).

For the moment, take the next right turn into **SANDLAND STREET**, where the **Three Cups** on the north side is a c.1900 building descended from a tavern built on Charterhouse land and recorded in 1472 as the 'Three Cuppes'. The frontage of the pub follows the line of Gray's Inn Passage, which once struck diagonally north-westwards to join with Red Lion Passage in providing a now lost pedestrian route through to Red Lion Square. **Three Cups Yard** survives, leading through an archway to the rear of the performing arts centre. The opposite side of Sandland Street consists (1998) of a large void resulting from the demolition of a huge office block on High Holborn named State House.

At **RED LION STREET**, continue straight ahead, but first look along its south end, lined by **New Century House** (named for the cleaning company once based there), Seifert's self-effacing **Lion House**, and the defiantly ugly **Allied Dunbar House**. On the far corner is the **Old Red Lion**, a 19th-century incarnation of the ancient tavern which gave the street its name. The 'Old' prefix was possibly added to distinguish this pub from a later one, at Nos.62-63 Red Lion Street, called the Red Lion *and Ball*.

Now continue along **EAGLE STREET**, one of the area's oldest streets and once one of its poorest. Martin van Butchell, born here c.1770, became a successful, if eccentric, quack doctor who rode the streets of the West End on a spotted pony, sporting a waist-length beard. Today almost all the buildings post-date WW II, and there is little that need detain us. The **Finnish Institute**, a self-consciously Nordic building at Nos.35-36, stands on the site of the 18th-century Eagle

brewhouse. Note the elephant plaque high up on the wall, whose significance is a mystery. Leading north into Red Lion Square is tiny **DANE STREET**. Originally Leigh (or Lee) Street, it later merged with Dean Street, its southward continuation (now buried beneath Sunley House), and bears a variant of its name. Land here has been owned since 1522 by the 'Holborn Charity' of the parish of St Clement Danes at the Aldwych. Passing **Yorkshire Grey Yard**, a diminutive access road recalling another lost pub, emerge into Procter Street, from where you may return to our starting point at Holborn Underground or, if you prefer, proceed to route 2.

## Route 2
# King's Gate to Queen Square

Again we begin at the Holborn Underground station, this time striking northwards on a linear walk to Queen Square. Cross High Holborn, keeping on the east side of Southampton Row, and then turn right into **CATTON STREET**, once the western end of Eagle Street, passing on the corner the **Baptist Church House** of 1903, designed by Arthur Keen. The Baptist Union has now moved out of London, leaving behind a statue of John Bunyan, set in a niche at first floor level, and accompanied by the opening words of *The Pilgrim's Progress*.

On the south side of Catton Street, surmounted by a cupola, is tiny **Kingsgate House**, formerly part of Kingsgate Baptist Chapel, founded in Eagle Street in 1735, and twice rebuilt, latterly in circular form. It once stood on the corner of Kingsgate Street, where Mrs Gamp (of *Martin Chuzzlewit*) lodged, next door to the mutton pie shop and opposite the cats' meat warehouse. Kingsgate Street, obliterated in 1902-6 by the LCC's Kingsway scheme, followed the line of the old royal highway already mentioned (p 16), which here ran north out of (High)

Holborn to join what is now Theobalds Road. At its south end stood a barrier called the King's Gate. Here in 1669, wrote Pepys, the royal coach was overturned, depositing Charles II and his companions in the road — a case, however, of 'all dirt and no hurt'. Two left turns lead us into short, featureless

**FISHER STREET**. It once housed a generating station of the Metropolitan Electricity Supply Co., designed so that its huge working dynamos could be admired from the pavement: the humming metal panels of today's substation are a poor substitute.

Turn right on returning to **SOUTHAMPTON ROW**, in all but name the north end of Edwardian Kingsway, which here absorbed the earlier, narrower, King Street. At the northern portal of the tramway tunnel, closed in 1952 and latterly used as a control centre for London's flood defences, tramlines remain set in the cobbled incline. **Carlisle House**, originally offices of the Royal London Friendly Society, and a fine example of the Arts & Crafts style, was renovated in 1997 after years of dereliction. Next door is the Central School of Arts & Crafts, founded by the LCC in 1896 and moved here from Regent Street 12 years later. A blue plaque commemorates William R Lethaby, the building's architect and the first principal of the school, now known, after a merger, as the **Central St Martin's College of Art & Design** (a constituent College of the London Institute). An offshoot of the school, adjoining it around the corner, and covering the site of the pre-WW II Theobalds Road fire station, is the (Jeannetta) **Cochrane Theatre** of 1963. Notice how the north façade of the school

tucks itself in behind the theatre, following the line of Orange (later Parton) Street, once another of the short diagonal approaches to Red Lion Square. No.4 Parton Street was before WW II a celebrated left-wing bookshop run by David Archer.

Cross to the north side of Theobalds Road, where the **White Hart** on the corner of Boswell Street was rebuilt on its original site after wartime destruction. Turn left along **OLD GLOUCESTER STREET**, dating from the early 18th century, and named after the Duke of Gloucester, longest-surviving son of Queen Anne, who unlike his 16 even sicklier siblings lived to the ripe old age of eleven, having spent time in our locality to benefit from the purity of the air. Old houses surviving on the west side include **No.44**, with a plaque commemorating the death here in 1781 of Bishop Richard Challoner, Vicar Apostolic to London's Catholics at a time of great bigotry against them. The previous year, during the Gordon Riots, ruffians called at No.44 to find that their prey had fled an hour before. An earlier Gloucester Street resident was Robert Nelson, a founder member of both the Society for Promoting Christian Knowledge and the Society for the Propagation of the Gospel. In 1822 the charismatic Rev. Edward Irving (p 82) stayed at No.19 on first arriving in London, in what he called 'good, elegant rooms' in an 'airy and healthy' area. Edward Fitzgerald (p 49) lived at No.15 in 1854.

More old houses, at **Nos.32-26**, face the secluded **Alf Barrett Playground**; then, set back from the street, comes **No.27**, a former factory which made motor accessories in 1907. At the north end of the street are the old St George the Martyr schools, now united in John's Mews (p 37). They have had a complicated history since 1708, when a school for 20 boys and 20 girls was established in the church's Vestry House. The boys moved to Cross (now Gage) Street in 1739, and on again in 1852 to the south side of Theobalds Road, their place in Cross Street being taken by the girls and infants who had meanwhile remained at Vestry House. A new building for 200 girls and 200 infants, opened in 1863, is now **Lundonia House**, incorporating the **October** (art) **Gallery**. When Theobalds Road was widened in 1878, the boys moved back to new premises next door to the church - 'ugly and gloomy Gothic' was Pevsner's verdict on this S S Teulon creation, now occupied by a private-sector college.

Turn right (east) along very narrow **GAGE STREET**. The renovated building on the left at the far end was before WW I the Brown Bear public house. Turn right into **BOSWELL STREET**, dating from the 1690s, and originally known as Devonshire Street, hence modern

**Devonshire Court**. Walk towards the south end, where on the east side **Richbell** flats stand opposite the site of Old Devonshire House, reputedly built in 1667 for the Earl, later 1st Duke, of Devonshire. It was destroyed in WW II, having latterly served as a music museum. Instruments which had wisely been evacuated from it may now be seen at Fenton House, Hampstead. Before he was 12, the poet Alexander Pope (b.1688) underwent part of his erratic schooling in Boswell Street at the mercy of a master whom he described as a 'Popish renegado'. No.29 was home from 1828 to William Brockedon, the artist, author and inventor, whose *Passes of the Alps* inspired Murray to publish his well-known Guides. Harold Monro ran a poetry bookshop in the street in 1913-26, and the poet Robert Frost took rooms above it in 1913 'by pure accident'. A painting room in (the then) Devonshire Street was rented in 1928 by Victor Pasmore, a co-founder of the Euston Road school of painting (*see also* p 82).

Before WW II, many poor Italians - organ grinders, ice cream vendors and chestnut sellers - still lived here, alongside a small colony of workers in gold, aluminium and brass. In the 19th century Devonshire Street is thought to have been one address of the Italian patriot Giuseppe Mazzini, who spent many years of exile lying low, quietly (and ineffectively) plotting the overthrow of Continental

autocrats. Ever cosmopolitan, Boswell Street today is almost wholly lined by 20th-century blocks of flats housing a high proportion of Bangladeshi residents.

Retrace your steps towards the north and glance briefly to the right into **BOSWELL COURT**, where the blue-and-white building was, in 1906, a factory making upholsterers' trimmings and bag frames. The footway was named, not after Johnson's biographer, but after Edward Boswell, a St Giles bricklayer and churchwarden who built houses here; the court lent its name to the adjoining street when the latter was renamed (from Devonshire Street) in 1937.

Now continue into tranquil **QUEEN SQUARE**. Built in 1706-1720 on land owned by Sir Nathaniel Curzon of Kedleston, it was known at first as Devonshire Square, though soon renamed in honour of Anne, the reigning queen. Originally aristocratic, it was home in 1728 to a peer and three bishops, and by mid-century to five peers of the realm. Figure 3 shows it, seen not from this end but from the northeast corner, in the early 19th century. Artists and intellectuals later colonised the square, but very few of their houses remain, most having been rebuilt,

*3 'Queen Square 1810', a misleadingly labelled impression from Old and New London (c.1873). On the left, porticoed Queen Square House.*

or replaced in the 19th century by hospitals, convents or places of education. Windsor lanterns atop the lamp-posts lend an air of antiquity to the square, as does a cast-iron pump in the paved-over roadway at the south end, where maids once queued to fill their jugs and pails.

Facing the pump is the former Italian Hospital, opened in 1884 by Giovanni (John) Ortelli in his own house, No.41, to serve his poorer immigrant countrymen. It later expanded into No.40 and a house round the corner in what is now Boswell Street. In 1898-9 a new building was erected, designed by T W Cutler in a Renaissance style, with a fine cupola topped by a gilded cross. Falling demand for beds led to the discharge of the last patient in 1989. Still boldly inscribed with the hospital's name, and with a version of the Italian royal arms above its door, the building is now the **Italian Wing** of the Hospital for Sick Children (p 31). Next door at **No.42** (once two imposing 18th-century houses), is the bustling **Mary Ward Centre** for adult education and community advice, removed here from Tavistock Place (p.50). The building previously housed evening classes of the ILEA's Stanhope Institute; earlier, the LCC Technical School for Women, whose curriculum included dressmaking, millinery and photography; and, before WW I, the Government School of Art for Ladies. Earlier still it was a temporary

home of the College of Preceptors, founded in 1846 as an examining body for teachers.

We now begin an anticlockwise tour of the square, passing, on the corner of Great Ormond Street, the offices of **York House**. The music historian Charles Burney lived at No.39, on this site, in 1771-2. His daughter Fanny, whose novel *Evelina* would appear in 1776, wrote of the 'beautiful prospect' from the house 'of the hills, ever verdant and smiling'. (The north end of the square had been left undeveloped to preserve the view northward, an amenity lost when the Foundling estate was built up.) The Burneys' visitors included Garrick and Goldsmith as well as Captain Cook, who dined here just before leaving on his second voyage of discovery, accompanied by Burney's son James. Charles' musical interests lived on in the square in the form of the Queen Square Select Society, devotees of Beethoven during the composer's lifetime. Richard Limpus, who founded the Royal College of Organists in 1864, lived at No.41.

Ignoring for the moment the west wing of the Homeopathic Hospital (p 00), walk north along the east side of Queen Square, all of whose 18th-century houses have given way to later buildings. One apparent survival (but actually rebuilt in Edwardian times after a fire) is tiny **No.33**, sandwiched endearingly between its bulkier

neighbours. Catherine wheels incised in its doorcase, and the inscription *In omnibus glorificetur Deus* above, recall the earlier occupation of Nos.32-33 by St Katherine's Convent. Noted for its School of Ecclesiastical Embroidery, it was run by an Anglican sisterhood, which in 1909 converted to Catholicism and decamped to Farnborough. Former No.31 housed the Aged Poor Society, and the Society of St Vincent de Paul (named after the patron saint of charitable institutions), which once supplied the nursing staff for the Italian Hospital. At No.29 was the Working Women's College, founded by Elizabeth Malleson in 1864 after failing to persuade its male counterpart (p 28) to admit females. Ironically, her own establishment was to become co-educational 10 years later as the College for Men & Women, under which name it closed in 1901.

Still on the east side, the mid-19th century saw the closure at former No.24 of a very different female education establishment, namely a prestigious private academy founded in the 18th century, and nicknamed the 'Ladies' Eton'. Fanny Burney and Veronica Boswell, daughter of James, were among its pupils. The girls worshipped at St George the Martyr, travelling the few yards to the church in a decrepit old carriage in order to practise getting in and out with due decorum. When the coach could no longer be moved, it was set up within the academy so that the girls could continue their lessons in propriety. It was *im*propriety that led to the sacking of the satirical poet Charles Churchill, a tutor at the school. Jerome K Jerome later lived in Queen Square for a while, probably at No.29, though the humorist himself could not be sure, having had 'no head for numbers'. Female education of a third kind took place at No.22, home in 1858-63 of the Ladies' Charity School previously in John Street (p. 40), which trained poor girls for domestic service.

In 1865 'The Firm', founded by William Morris and others in Red Lion Square, moved to No.26, with workshops in a converted ballroom at the rear. Morris, weary of daily commuting from the wilds of Kent, moved into the house with his wife and children. Although he wrote here his *Earthly Paradise*, he would not have described the square as such, for he never enjoyed living here, and in 1872 moved with his family to west of Hammersmith. His by then flourishing business stayed at No.26 for a further 9 years before relocating to Merton Abbey.

All these houses gave way to what is now called the **National Hospital for Neurology & Neurosurgery**. It was founded in 1859, on the initiative of the Chandlers, a middle-class St Pancras family whose grandmother had suffered a stroke, with support from David Wire, then Lord Mayor of London, and himself

the victim of a minor neurological attack. Originally the National Hospital for the Paralysed and Epileptics, it later became the National Hospital for Nervous Diseases. Opened at No.24 with just eight beds for females, it soon expanded into neighbouring houses. Purpose-built accommodation followed in 1885, when the older of its two blocks was erected, in red brick and terracotta by Simpson & Manning. Known for a time as the 'Albany Memorial', it bears a stone in memory of Leopold, Duke of Albany. The plain extension of 1937, with balconies on which patients could take the air, was financed by public subscription, but named the Rockefeller Wing after the American foundation which sponsored the hospital's research. There is a foundation stone laid by Princess Alice of Athlone, longest surviving grand-daughter of Queen Victoria, and reliefs affirming the institution's dual objectives of 'research' and 'healing'. Pioneering the active treatment of nervous disorders, the National rapidly gained an international reputation, and has since expanded to take over a considerable proportion of the square.

The flats of **Queen Court** were built in the 1930s on the till then undeveloped north side of the square. Next door, at **No.23**, are the former headquarters and laboratories of the Royal Institute of Public Health & Hygiene (founded 1931), whose

*4   The 'Devil's Conduit' at 20 Queen Square, photographed c.1910. Steps lead down to tunnels beneath the garden.*

name is still prominently inscribed. Beyond is a footway leading out of the square into Guilford Street, past a small garden and an entrance to the underground car park of the President Hotel. On the west side stood No.21 Queen Square, home in 1846-56 of the Dissenting theologian, founder of Christian Socialism and social reformer F D Maurice (and co-founder, 1854, of the Working Men's College, see p 28; and No.20, the house of Dr John Campbell, to which Dr Johnson repaired on a Sunday evening for conversation, though troubled by the 'shoals of Scotsmen who flocked about'. Later occupants included Edmond Hoyle, the 18th-century expert on whist; Louisa Twining, the poor-law and workhouse reformer, who raised eyebrows by sheltering homeless women in her house; and the architect Thomas Wyatt. By 1907 No.20 had become a Quaker institute. Accessed through a trap-door in the back garden were the stonework tunnels from a source feeding a medieval conduit we shall encounter again in Rugby Street (p 33). Known initially as the Devil's Conduit (Fig 4; diabolic names were given to anything novel or strange), and by the 18th century as the Chimney Conduit (after the shape of the conduit head), it survived until 1911-3, when the house was replaced by Turkish baths for ladies. These in turn were demolished c.1960. In adjacent Queen Square Place, built a few years later than

the square on land owned by the Earl of Salisbury and originally named Brunswick Row, two lords and a general once lived as neighbour. It is now only the goods entrance of Russell Square's Imperial Hotel.

On the west side of Queen Square is **Alexandra House** at **No.17**, once the Alexandra Hospital for Poor Children with Hip Disease. As the House of Relief for Children with Chronic Disease of the Joints, it was founded in 1867 to meet a problem then prevalent in working-class children. The present building, by Marshall & Vicars (1899), served the hospital for 21 years until it moved to Swanley. It later housed a Fighter Control Unit of the Royal Auxiliary Air Force, before conversion to offices in 1960. 18th-century houses survive, though much altered, at **Nos.14-16**, the latter a home for working boys c.1907-1925. **St John's House** at **No.12** was a base for the sisterhood of St John & St Thomas, an Anglican nursing order, which in 1906 moved into Queen Square from Norfolk, bringing their 50-year-old convent with them. Individually numbered stones are said to have been used to erect a replica of their former premises. St John's House later served as a home for night nurses at distant St Thomas' Hospital, was taken over by the National Hospital in 1967, and renovated in 1995 as a 'functional imaging centre'. Carefully preserved are reliefs

depicting an eagle, and a snake in a chalice, both symbols of St John, as well as a small statue of the evangelist with a tiny version of the cupped serpent in his hand.

**Nos.8-11**, designed by Andrew Prentice in a somewhat French style, were built in 1909 as joint examination halls of the Royal Colleges of Physicians and of Surgeons, a role which lasted until the 1980s. Now named **Charles Symonds House** (after an ex-president of the Association of British Neurologists), this building too is a part of the National Hospital, but the coats-of-arms of the two Royal Colleges still adorn the façade. In 1865-73 former No.8, on this site, housed Dr Williams's Library of nonconformist literature, now in Gordon Square. At **No.6** is an 18th-century survival which since 1913 has been the headquarters of the Art Workers' Guild, founded in 1884 by a merger of two groups of young artists, whose members included W R Lethaby and Walter Crane. The site of No.5, home to the National Pharmaceutical Union until the 1950s, is covered by **No.3**, modern headquarters of the publishers Faber & Faber, whose concrete and glass is out of character with everything else in the square. **No.2**, by contrast, is of the later 18th century and has an attractive iron balcony. The **Queen's Larder** pub at No.1 dates, as a building, from c.1710. There is a story that George III once stayed in the square for private treatment by his physician, and that his devoted wife Charlotte rented a cellar here, beneath what was then an unnamed beershop, to store culinary delights for his comfort. Evidence for the King's stay is unfortunately both scant and inconsistent.

The **gardens** of Queen Square, maintained by Camden Council, are open to the public by agreement with the Council, but closed for one day each year to maintain their private status, as evidenced by the badges of the National and children's hospitals which each surmount one of its gateways. At the south end, a floral bowl celebrates the Queen's Silver Jubilee of 1977, as do lines by Philip Larkin and Ted Hughes set in the paving alongside. Two benches commemorate the death of 16 homoeopathic doctors in the Trident air disaster of 1972. Easily missed, set in the lawn north-east of the central pathway, is a small plaque marking the spot where a bomb landed during a night-time Zeppelin raid in 1915, without loss of life even though 1000 people were asleep in their beds around the square at the time. During WW II twice that number slept in a shelter under the gardens.

Nearby is a sculpture (unveiled 1997) representing Humphry, the Mary Ward Centre's house cat, named presumably after Mary's husband! A cat may look at a king, but this one looks towards the north end of the gardens and the leaden statue of a queen, erected in 1775 and paid for by Mr Oliver Becket, a resident. The lady's identity is controversial. Caroline and Mary II have been suggested as (unlikely) candidates; the Victorians believed her to be Anne. But the modern consensus, as a plaque indicates, is that she is Charlotte. In his *London Statues*, Arthur Byron unkindly concludes that 'the face of the statue is pretty, which should eliminate them all, especially Charlotte'.

At the south-west corner of Queen Square is the church of **St George the Martyr**, predating the actual square, and built by private subscription in 1706 as a chapel of ease for the residents of this then new suburb. In 1723 it was promoted to parochial status, and an early rector was William Stukeley, an antiquarian whose (erroneous) theories on Stonehenge earned him the nickname of 'Arch-Druid'. In 1868 the originally plain church was radically altered by Teulon, who plastered its walls, and replaced its previously squat bell tower with a curiously shaped zinc-clad steeple; carved symbols of the four evangelists occupy circular niches in the east wall. St George's is sometimes known as the 'sweeps' church', because of the annual Christmas dinner provided there by Captain James South's Charity for 100 chimney sweeps' apprentices, until the use of climbing boys was outlawed in 1875.

**COSMO PLACE** is a lively footway leading west to Southampton Row. Catering largely for the inner man, it offers two restaurants and two pubs of some antiquity, the **Swan** dating back to at least 1757. The paved western end lies just within the Duke of Bedford's Bloomsbury estate, hence its name (*see panel, p21*), and was called Fox Court until it merged with the cobbled eastern part, originally known as Little Ormond Street. The Bloomsbury Park Hotel covers the site of two Georgian houses called Rector's Glebe, as their rents were paid to the incumbent of the neighbouring parish church. Their ground floors were eventually converted into shops; it was above a baker's at No.12 that conductor (Sir) John Barbirolli was born in 1899 of Italian-French parents. A blue plaque in his honour faces the main road (Southampton Row), into which we may turn right to walk north to Russell Square and its Underground station (second turning on the right). Alternatively, return to Queen Square for the start of route 3.

## Route 3
# Mostly The Rugby Estate

In 1567, a field named Conduit Close was donated to Rugby School (Warwickshire) by its founder, Lawrence Sheriff. Although it has disposed of many freeholds over the years, the school still owns much property in this locality, and the Rugby estate is the subject of most of this circular walk from Russell Square Underground station. Turn left from the station, then left again along Herbrand Street and, crossing Guilford Street, follow one of the pathways almost opposite into Queen Square.

At its far (south) end, turn left into **GREAT ORMOND STREET**. The nearest stretch, dating from the 1680s, was named Ormond Street (after the Duke of Ormonde, Charles I's viceroy in Ireland) for two centuries, before merging with its eastern end to form a freshly numbered Great Ormond Street.

18th-century Ormond Street was a very desirable address, the sizeable houses on its north side having had very long gardens backing onto open country. Early residents included, in 1746, the Earl of Hardwick, Lord High Steward who presided at the trials of the Jacobite lords after the 1745 rebellion. Lord Thurlow, a widely

unpopular ("vulgar, arrogant, profane and immoral") Lord Chancellor under several Administrations, was living at erstwhile No.45 in 1784, when thieves broke into his study and made off with the Great Seal of England. Never recovered, it had to be remade. Thomas Babington Macaulay, also a lawyer, but better known for his historical works, lived in 1823 at old

---

### Street names along route 3 and their origin

**Barbon**
Dr Nicholas, late 17th-century property speculator

**Lamb's Conduit**
Water supply to the City, financed by William Lambe

**Millman**
Sir William Milman/Millman of (Great) Ormond Street

**Orde Hall**
John, member of the Holborn District Board, Metropolitan Board of Works

**Ormond**
1st Duke of Ormonde, royalist Civil War commander

**Powis**
William Herbert, 2nd Marquis of Powis, built Powis House

**Rugby**
Local land endows Rugby School

---

No.50, the home of his father Zachary, before taking chambers in Gray's Inn. No.49 was home to Dr Richard Mead (d. 1754), a royal physician of great repute and chief physician to the Foundling Hospital (p 41), to consult whom the consumptive painter Watteau travelled specially from Paris.

As the gentry migrated westwards, institutions moved in. Old No.40, on the north side, was home in the 1860s to the Lincoln's Inn & Temple Charity School. In 1857 the Working Men's College moved from Red Lion Square (p 15) into Lord Thurlow's old house at No.45, later expanding into No.44 next door (Fig 5), before moving on to Crowndale Road in 1906. F D Maurice (p 26), the first principal, was succeeded by Thomas Hughes, author of *Tom Brown's Schooldays*. The Catholic Church of St John of Jerusalem adjoined, at Nos.46-47, the RC Hospital of SS John & Elizabeth, founded in 1856 by Cardinal Wiseman to serve the sick poor. Though all these establishments are long gone, two hospitals remain. At the western end is the **Royal London Homeopathic Hospital**, its royal prefix added by command of George VI. Founded in Golden Square in 1849, it moved into a house in Great Ormond Street 10 years later. The purpose-built premises of 1893-5 were designed by W A Pite, with a curious jumble of motifs. The more harmonious Sir Henry Tyler Wing

*5   Hall in Working Men's College, which was at 44-45 Great Ormond Street from 1857 to 1906. A poster already announces a lecture on the college's history.*

(1909), on the corner of Queen Square, was the work of E T Hall, also architect of the plain (now derelict) Nurses' Home opposite.

**Powis Place**, now only an ambulance road, occupies the site of palatial Powis House (Fig 6), built c1700 for William Herbert, the 2nd Marquis of Powis, who was once sent to the Tower as an alleged Jacobite sympathiser. His mansion later became the French embassy, but burned down in 1714, possibly as a result of arson. Louis XIV paid for its reconstruction, which wisely included a reservoir on the roof, doubling as a fishpond and as a water supply in case of another fire. Serving as the Spanish embassy in 1864-83, the house was demolished soon after, and a street of smaller houses was built on the site. John Leech, the caricaturist, *Punch* contributor and friend of Thackeray, lived here at No.6 prior to 1854, next door to a home for 'friendless girls'. At the bottom of the long garden of Powis House, on the banks of the Fleet tributary, were Powis Wells, an extensively patronised but never fashionable spa, complete with pump room and pleasure gardens. Its buildings were later converted to serve as a sanatorium for sick children at the Foundling Hospital (p 41).

30

The world-famous **Great Ormond Street Hospital for Sick Children** was founded in 1851, when most hospitals granted admission to young children only exceptionally. One, for example, admitted under-sevens only for amputations. Dr Charles West, with some colleagues, rented Dr Mead's old house at No.49 and opened with just 10 beds in 1852. Six years later, No.48 was acquired, and a new neo-Gothic building designed by E M Barry, was started in 1872, covering the long back gardens of the two houses. It opened 5 years later, and was followed by a further new block in 1893. Complete rebuilding, with Stanley Hall as architect, was completed in 1938. Expansion and reconstruction have continued ever since, helped by J M Barrie's well-known gift to the hospital in 1929 of all future royalties from performances of *Peter Pan*.

The **School of Nursing**, a featureless modern block lining much of the north side of Great Ormond Street, replaced a series of late Victorian 'chambers' blocks, including Norton Chambers, home in the 1890s to William Archer, the Scottish drama critic and translator of Ibsen; and Leigh Chambers, where the painter Wyndham Lewis set up his short-lived Rebel Art School in 1914.

*6   Powis House (1700-1885)*
*'in Ormond Street', drawn by Sutton Nicholls.*

On the south side, **Nos.41-61** form a continuous row of early 18th-century houses, which some believe may have been started by Dr Barbon. In 1877 at **Nos.55-57** William Morris founded the Society for the Protection of Ancient Buildings, which remained here until it moved to Spitalfields c.1980. Morris and his wife Jane had lived as newly-weds at old No.41 on the other side of the road, while awaiting completion of their 'Red House' at Bexleyheath in 1859. **No.49** has an attractive doorway, and a wooden front that is probably a product of its late Victorian role as a coffee tavern. The porches of **Nos.41-43** have interesting Ionic columns and segmental pediments. No.41 was occupied in 1915-39 by the West Central Collegiate School, a long-surviving 'dame school' (of the superior kind) previously in Mecklenburgh Square (p 46). **Nos.43-45** (with Corinthian pilasters) are occupied by medical charities, respectively Leukaemia Research and the Migraine Trust.

Beyond Orde Hall Street (p.00), more early houses remain at **Nos.21-27**, with some agreeable Victorian shop fronts. **No.27** once housed the UK Benefit Society, founded in 1828; 90 years later rooms here were rented by Saxon Sydney-Turner, Treasury mandarin and Bloomsbury Group member. A blue plaque at **No.23** identifies the home (1777-90) of the prison reformer John Howard who was, however, travelling widely in Britain and Europe at the time, comparing penal systems.

East of Lamb's Conduit Street, in what was originally New Ormond Street, most houses date from 1710-20, **No.7** boasting a fine doorcase and Queen Anne hood; but **No.2** is early Victorian. Faced with a huge maintenance bill for the large number of Grade II listed buildings it owned, mostly occupied by tenants paying low, controlled rents, the Rugby estate sold 42 of them in 1977 to Camden Council for rehabilitation. A plaque on the south side commemorates the restoration in 1980 of **Nos.1-15**. The economist John Maynard Keynes, another of the Bloomsbury Set's less artistically inclined members, lived at **No.10** in 1914.

At **MILLMAN STREET**, turn left. At this southern end, begun c1690 on the Rugby estate, are modern flats, and two terraces of heavy, late-Victorian houses now restored by the Council. In 1812 John Bellingham, a disgruntled Liverpudlian bankrupt, lodged in the street before making his way to the lobby of the House of Commons to assassinate the prime minister, Spencer Perceval. Neo-Gothic architect S S Teulon lived at erstwhile No.18 in 1841; and Gerald Brenan (also p 37) lodged at No.10 when he first arrived in London and took to writing. The northern end of the street (once New Millman Street) was completed only in 1803, and lay on the Foundling estate, into which we now briefly stray. An early resident was the transvestite Chevalier D'Eon, sometime soldier, diplomat, master swordsman and secret agent of Louis XVI. Disabled by a wound sustained in a fencing accident, he spent his twilight years at No.26 New Millman Street in the guise of a woman. When he died in poverty in 1810, and his body was medically examined, neighbours were astonished to learn that the person they knew as the 'Chevalière' was really a man. Two early houses survive at **Nos.60-62** Millman Street. **MILLMAN MEWS**, opposite, is a cul-de-sac leading only to what was once the Doughty Garage.

Turn left along Guilford Street, and through Guilford Place (p 43), to reach **LAMB'S CONDUIT STREET**. On the corner of the **Lamb** public house are parish boundary marks, 'SPP' for St Pancras, into which former parish we have fleetingly trespassed; and 'SAH' for St Andrew Holborn, which we now re-enter. Dating from c.1779, the pub was once known as the Lion & Lamb. Its Victorian incarnation was well restored in 1961, the fine tiled front, internal woodwork and engraved glass, and the 'snob screens' at the bar being retained. The Lamb was frequented by various members of the Bloomsbury Group, and in Virginia Woolf's *Jacob's Room*, the eponymous habitation is either in or very near Lamb's Conduit Street.

Glance into **Long Yard**, where **Nos.4-5**

once housed a cab and coach builder, and a farrier. By the yard entrance, in the wall of modern **Rokeby House**, an eroded old plaque declares that 'Lamb's Conduit is the property of the City of London. This pump is erected for the benefit of the Publick.' In 1577 William Lambe, a wealthy member of the Clothworkers' Company, paid £1500 for the renovation of an old conduit house at Snow Hill dating from 1498. Lead pipes were laid to bring water there, by way of Leather Lane, from a dammed Fleet tributary and from some of its associated springs. It was here near Long Yard that the water was captured for use by local people and a pump was provided by the public-spirited City fathers, possibly fed from a reservoir rediscovered in 1851 in the cellar of former No.88 Lamb's Conduit Street. Although the importance of the conduit diminished when the New River was opened in 1613, many people compared the purity of the local water favourably with that of the Hertfordshire commodity. Rebuilt in 1736, the conduit survived only a further decade before demolition. The stone effigy of a lamb which had adorned the conduit head later served as the inn sign of the Lamb tavern. Today, the ram trademark of Young's brewery is, confusingly, more in evidence. Opposite are the Camelia Botnar laboratories, whose controversial development was conditional on renovation of the façade of listed **No.83**

next door, previously Mel Calman's Cartoon Gallery.

The semi-pedestrianised central section of the street retains something of a 'high street' atmosphere, though many shops supplying everyday needs have given way to more specialised and up-market outlets. The Sun public house, of the early 19th century, though much altered, was renamed the **Finnegan's Wake** in 1995, simply an Irish title for another 'theme pub'; James Joyce had no local associations. A number of listed 18th-century houses have survived, with a pleasing variety of later shop fronts. Most of the houses have served a number of purposes over the decades. The florist's at **No.29**, inscribed '1887', was successively a chandler's, a dairy and a boot repairer's; **No.35**, adorned with little lions' heads, was selling motor accessories in 1906, but had previously been a home for working boys; the dental surgery at **No.41** was once a signwriter's; **No.43** (c1700-1715, though much altered), has been occupied by a bootmaker, a patent medicine maker, and oil and colour men; while Doric-pilastered **No.51** has served too many trades for us to list. An archway next to No.55a leads into **Lamp Office Court** which, as early as 1702, was a local base of the Conic Lighting Company, one of two firms then contracted to light the streets in the more affluent parts of London, and whose whale-oil lamps, though dismal by modern standards, were the envy of visiting foreigners.

In summer, eating places spill on to the pavement in Lamb's Conduit Street, lending a Continental air (somewhat marred by the frequent presence of litter) to what has long been a cosmopolitan area. The Conduit Coffee House was for generations a café run by the Italian Domenidietti family. 'Founded 1843', proclaims an inscription facing it at **No.64**, referring presumably to the United Patriots National Benefit Society, one of the six similar bodies created in the earlier 19th century to provide sickness cover and life assurance for ordinary people. It was based here for over a century, and was indeed founded in 1843, in what is now North Gower Street. The name, date and accompanying motif (a bundle of *fasces*) combine to suggest an Italian expatriate connection.

Turn left into **RUGBY STREET**, dating from c.1700, and known until 1936 as Chapel Street. Narrow, two-storey **No.20**, in dark red brick, was once (as No.19 Chapel Street), the entrance to the Church of Humanity, alias Positivist School, opened in 1870 by Richard Congreve and fellow disciples of the French philosopher Auguste Comte. Ritualistic 'services' took place in a room to the rear, where people of all social classes met in praise of humanity, surrounded by busts of the great and the

good of human history. The 'Religion of Humanity' had its own calendar of 13 months, with feast days honouring secular 'saints' from Socrates to Shelley, from Ptolemy to Priestley, from Romulus to Rossini. Dwindling support led to closure of the 'church' c1932, and its premises soon became a dance hall. Renamed **'Buckingham House'**, they now house financial consultants. 18th-century **Nos.10-16** on the north side, with white porches, and hoods on carved brackets, are further beneficiaries of Camden Council renovation. **No.18** is Victorian, but boasts a Georgian doorcase.

**Rugby Chambers** (1867) at No.2 was built on the site of the self-styled Episcopal Chapel of St John, which had given the street its original name, and was shown as 'The Chapell' on a map of 1702. Although it was never consecrated, its pulpit attracted several eminent Anglican preachers, and William Wilberforce was numbered among its congregation. From 1827 the resident preacher was the Rev. Baptist Wriothesley Noel, a fervent evangelical. In 1848 he abandoned the Chapel, which was demolished, and two years later lived up to his forename by converting to the Baptist faith, serving for 18 years as minister at nearby John Street (p 39). The **Rugby Tavern** on the opposite corner was created in the mid-19th- century by knocking together two houses of the early 18th century.

Also on the south side of the street, **No.13** was until recently the popular French's Dairy, whose attractive tiled shop front and fascia have been preserved, together with an old plaque stating that 'In the rear is the White Conduit (circa 1300 AD), originally part of the water supply to the Greyfriars' monastery, Newgate Street'. Identified a century ago, the conduit head still exists behind what is now a shop selling *objets d'art*. Edwardian antiquarians concluded that the lead-piped conduit predated 1258, and that the spring here was one of two which fed it, the other being north of what became Queen Square (p 26). This White Conduit is not to be confused with a later, better-known namesake which ran from Islington to Charterhouse.

An archway nearby leads through a very narrow 18th-century passageway called **Emerald Court**. After burrowing through it, follow the footway on the right, turn left at Lamb's Conduit Street, right along Dombey Street (p 18), and right again into **ORDE HALL STREET**. Dating from 1882, this was built on land acquired cheaply for slum clearance by the Metropolitan Board of Works. It supplanted the notorious Little Ormond Yard, which had been described as a 'dangerous and disreputable haunt of Irish beggars and thieves', although contemporary census returns suggest that this was both a racist slur and a gross exaggeration. A night school for the education of the local poor, established in the yard in 1848 by the Working Men's College, would have had to compete with the pleasures of the Coach & Horses pub, opened some 5 years later. Built in yellow stock brick, the new street was once perfectly symmetrical, with terraces of modest houses on either side with decorative keystones over the doorways, and more substantial houses of greater pretension at each corner. Of the latter, three survive, as does the eastern terrace, restored by Camden Council in 1976, the terrace on the west side having been demolished after WW II.

Turn left along a footpath leading west past the post-WW II council flats of 14-storey **Chancellor's Court** and **Babington Court**. You are now actually passing through erstwhile (Great) Ormond Yard (Fig 7). This mews area, where William Morris once rented space, had by 1950 become a 'mouldering slum' begging for demolition. It is now a wilderness of tarmac and grass, its western egress, ahead of us, renamed **Ormond Close**. Turn right, however, into **BARBON CLOSE** (another modern re-naming), where the Victorian building on the right, now occupied by electrical engineers, was until the 1920s a mission hall and working men's club of the nearby parish church, witness the inscription '1876' and (beneath the chimneystack) the monogram 'St GM'.

We emerge at the north end through a square-cut archway, past a grubby signboard advertising 'George Bailey & Sons, horse and motor contractors', whose business flourished in the yard behind until after WW II. Listed as carmen (or carters) in the horse-drawn era, they later progressed to motorised road haulage; the sign must date from a transitional period.

A left turn along Great Ormond Street leads back to Queen Square, whence you may retrace your earlier steps northward to Russell Square Tube station.

*7  A late-17th-century house in erstwhile Ormond Yard, thought to have been the last galleried dwelling-house in London (photographed before WW II).*

# Route 4
# Largely The Doughty Estate

From Chancery Lane Underground station (closed on Sundays) turn west up High Holborn, and take the third right, along narrow **BROWNLOW STREET**. Bordering Gray's Inn, this was built by William Brownlow (d1675) on land in the manor of Portpool owned by his family since the previous century. His daughter Elizabeth married into the Doughty family, who in time became landlords of the estate that is the subject of this walk. In 1826 the family became extinct and the land passed to their relatives the Tichbornes.

An early-19th-century pump stands where Brownlow Street meets L-shaped Bedford Row. Veer briefly to the right to glance along **JOCKEY'S FIELDS**, the old mews area for the east side of the Row. The mews and its parent street were built c.1716-1720 on a 3-acre plot known as the Jockey Field. Bebbington's *London Street Names* suggests that this could have been where horses were prepared for an annual ceremonial ride by the Lord Mayor and Aldermen of the City of London to inspect the City Conduit (off Oxford Street). The name is now all that is of interest in this former mews area, where the blank

## Street names along route 4 and their origin

**Bedford**
Land locally endows the Bedford Charity
**Brownlow**
Elizabeth (fl.1675) married into the Doughty family
**Doughty**
Henry, of Bedford Row, wealthy local landowner (fl.1792)
**James**
James Burgess, associate of George Brownlow Doughty
**Jockey's**
A local field had various equestrian associations
**John**
John Blagrave, carpenter to the Doughty family
**King's**
Theobalds Road was once a private royal highway, the King's Way
**Northington**
Robert Henley, Earl of Northington, 1760s Lord Chancellor
**Roger**
Renaming of Henry Street, significance unknown
**Theobalds**
Hertfordshire hunting park of the Stuart kings

wall of Gray's Inn faces on to a west side damaged in WW II and substantially rebuilt. Replacement of the cobbled roadway with insensitive tarmac and yellow lines has robbed the Fields of any residual charm they may have had.

Let us rather turn westward, then north, into broad and tree-lined **BEDFORD ROW** — named, of course, not after the Dukes of Bedford but after the charity whose estate we explored in Route 1, and on whose eastern boundary it lies. The east and south end, however, were on Brownlow-Doughty land, and most of the Row was developed by the Doughty family in the early 18th century. The east side, which is largely intact, presents many fine doorways, with early Georgian horizontal hoods and elegant fanlights. On the west side, which fared less well during WW II, many of the buildings are replacements in a fairly sympathetic neo-Georgian style. The Row was described in 1734 as 'one of the most noble streets that London has to boast of'. Elizabeth Cromwell, daughter of Oliver, died here aged 82 in 1731. At the Crown Coffee House, which flourished in the Row c.1724-44, the rules of whist were first drawn up. Henry Addington, born nearby in 1757, was to become the 1st Viscount Sidmouth, the uncompromising Home Secretary at the time of the Peterloo massacre (1819). John Abernethy, the eccentric surgeon who founded the medical school at St Bartholomew's

hospital (c.1781), lived at **No.14**, which later became offices of the Masonic Union.

The profession which had so resented Dr Barbon's intrusion into the area (p 13) was quick to colonise the resulting streets, and to this day the Row remains largely a preserve of solicitors and barristers.

*The Bedford Row Conspiracy* was a humorous story by Thackeray, published in 1840. Lawyers by then shared the Row with institutions of various kinds: the Entomological Society, founded in 1833 at **No.12**, the Lord's Day of Rest Association at **No.13**, and the Ironmongers' Association at No.48. The British Printing Industries Federation moved into **No.11** in 1938, later absorbing adjacent war-damaged **No.10**. Said to have been the finest house in the Row, No.11 (Fig 8) was home after 1776 to the landlord Henry Doughty himself. At Edwardian **Bank Chambers** (No.24), the 'ULB' monogram above the door recalls their former occupation by the Union of London Bank, later merged into the National Provincial.

Cross Theobalds Road at the zebra crossing and proceed along **GREAT JAMES STREET**, Bedford Row's narrower, treeless continuation, where solicitors' offices abound. Among the best preserved of local streets, and another feast

8    *The staircase of 11 Bedford Row, once home to Henry Doughty (photographed 1964).*

of hoods and fanlights, it was built from c.1721 by George Brownlow Doughty and his wife Frances, in association with one James Burgess. At **No.6** is a splendid mahogany porch, graced by a frieze of delicately carved festooned urns. **No.15**, headquarters of the Federation of Master Builders, was home in 1872-3 to Theodore Watts-Dunton, solicitor to D G Rossetti, minor poet, and a camp-follower of the Pre-Raphaelites. A neighbour at **No.3** was the poet Algernon Charles Swinburne, who spent two periods here in the 1870s. When Watts-Dunton first called with a letter of introduction, he surprised Swinburne in a state of undress, and was chased onto the pavement by a furious naked poet, but nevertheless befriended the poet and set about rescuing him from his life of debauchery.

Literary connections abound in Great James Street. Novelist George Meredith lived in the 1840s at his father's house, **No.26**; E V Lucas, who edited Charles Lamb and wrote for *Punch*, was at **No.5** in the 1890s and Frank Swinnerton, critic and writer of London-set novels, lived at **No.4**. From 1923-30 Leonard Woolf worked at **No.38** as literary editor of *The Nation*, while Francis and Vera Meynell ran their Nonesuch Press across the road at **No.16**, in partnership with the writer David Garnett, author of *Pocahontas* (1933). His friend Gerald Brenan, the novelist and Hispanophile, lived at **No.14**

in 1927-9, in what he described as 'the most beautiful street in London'. He contrasted the glory of the fine panelled staircases with his small attic flat and its '18th-century fireplace full of mousetraps'. Detective-story writer Dorothy L Sayers settled at **No.24** in 1921, staying for over 20 years. Today's **Nos.24-25** are a modern reconstruction, but incorporate a striking 18th-century doorcase, with a phoenix-adorned segmental pediment, brought here from long-demolished No.30 on the north side of Great Ormond Street (p 31).

Turning right into Northington Street, we pass the end of **COCKPIT YARD**, on the site of a fashionable 18th-century cockfighting venue, described in 1816 as the only remaining London cockpit still 'having any vogue'. A Victorian musical instrument warehouse in turn gave way to what are now the **Cockpit Workshops** of Camden Council. In **NORTHINGTON STREET** itself, old houses remain at **Nos.17-21**, but **Nos.18-20** opposite are a recent pastiche. The **Dickens** public house, a 20th-century rebuild, assumed that name only in the late 1980s, having been the White Lion for nearly two centuries. *Al fresco* drinkers sit at tables in the roadway of the few remaining yards of Kirk Street, a row of late Victorian tenements which ran north to join Roger Street before WW II.

A little way into **JOHN'S MEWS** on your right a white concrete building was

still signed as 'Holborn Assembly Hall' a decade after its closure (1987). During WW II this was the local Civil Defence headquarters. Holborn Library, whose back entrance is at the far end of this cul-de-sac, was itself built on what had been a Civil Defence training ground. In the northern (left) part of John's Mews, beyond modern **School House**, the inter-War flats of **Mytre Court** face onto the latest (1970s) incarnation of the peripatetic **St George the Martyr C of E Primary School**, here on its fourth site, and now geographically separated from its mother parish.

Continue east along Northington Street, past a low Dutch-gabled building bearing stone plaques dated 1903, and erected by members of the Finch family. At first a coach builders', it later became a garage, and was converted to flats in 1997. Opposite stands a curious Tudorish building, which begins with two storeys, and rises to four, presumably to match the height of adjacent No.28 John St. Although once numbered (as No.12), it was never separately listed in any ratebook, and seems to have been simply a late-Victorian side extension, built in the garden of its Georgian neighbour. Messrs Shrigley & Hunt, a firm of glass painters here in 1904, would doubtless have appreciated the generous natural light offered by the large oriel windows.

At the junction with John Street (p 39)

is the **King's Arms**, retaining a typical 19th-century wooden pub front. Continue eastward as Northington Street drops gently towards the Fleet valley. Two old wooden shop fronts are worth a second glance, especially the slightly bowed window at **No.8**. Ahead lies a strip of land, west of Gray's Inn Road, which in Victorian times became an industrial enclave. The workshops which colonised local mews were joined by a handful of small purpose-built factories, including Lachenal's concertina works at No.4, and at No.2 a surgical truss maker's, still operating in 1942. A probable major customer, with offices in nearby Great James Street, was the Rupture Society, whose main objective was the 'gratuitous provision of trusses'. **No.3**, with ground floor windows barred against thieves, was once devoted to scientific instrument making, an occupation much associated with the Italian community.

**KING'S MEWS**, approaching from the south, continues northwards as **NORTH MEWS**, for many years home to Jacob's sanitary ware factory, and along which we turn. North Mews is, in turn, continued by **BROWNLOW MEWS**, but we now turn left up **ROGER STREET**, originally named Henry Street after Henry Doughty, an association lost when it was re-named in 1937. Here around 1900 were a printers' ink works serving the staple industry of the locality, and Dr Tibble's chocolate factory.

Imagine the heady mix of aromas which must have permeated these streets from both that and the nearby Reid's brewery in Clerkenwell Road! The slightly winding street follows the line of the much-mentioned Fleet river tributary, forming part of the boundary between Holborn and St Pancras parishes, and their successor boroughs. Again crossing John Street, we pass on the right a wall-mounted boundary plate. Continue ahead to the **Duke of York** pub, rebuilt on its original site at the foot of John's Mews (p 37). Here turn right into **DOUGHTY MEWS**, a tastefully renovated backwater put to a mixture of residential and commercial uses, where **No.20** appears to have preserved three original double-leaved stable doors.

At the far end, turn right along Guilford Street, staying on the south side, and pausing where it meets **DOUGHTY STREET**. Despite its overall uniform appearance, this wide street was built gradually over 30 years, beginning in 1792, when its development by Henry Doughty (as Upper John Street) was prompted by the Foundling estate's eastern extension of Guilford Street over Doughty land. Notice the wide variety of styles in the railings and fanlights. To your left is a short section of Doughty Street running to the north of Guilford Street into

Mecklenburgh Square. Nos.20-28 on the west side were destroyed in WW II, and replaced by part of London House (p 44). Gothic revivalist architect William Butterfield lived in 1848-54 at No.24, in a street popular with architects. Though **Nos.32-38** opposite survived the war and are original, their neighbours at **Nos.29-31** are faithful reconstructions. **No.29** served in 1891 as Fellowship House, headquarters of the Fellowship of the New Life, an early socialist experiment in communal living, whose joint secretaries at that time were Edith Lees (the future bride of Havelock Ellis) and Ramsay MacDonald, then newly arrived in London. *From Doughty Street to Downing Street* is the title of Herbert Tracey's 1924 biography of the first Labour prime minister. (Baroness) Dr Edith Summerskill, a later Labour politician, was born in Doughty Street in 1901.

Turn southward along either side of Doughty Street. The journalist Edmund Yates, who lived in 1860 at **No.43**, on the east side, described the street as 'none of your common thoroughfares to be rattled through by vulgar cabs and earth-shaking Pickford vans, but a self-including property with a gate at each end, and a lodge with a porter in a gold-laced hat, with the Doughty arms on the buttons of his coat', preventing those not on business from 'intruding on the exclusive territory'. **No.48** was, in 1837-9, the first marital home of Charles Dickens, shared not only with wife Kate and son Charles, but also brother Fred and sister-in-law Mary Hogarth who, after a trip to theatre, expired here in the novelist's arms. Here he wrote *Oliver Twist* and most of *Nicholas Nickleby*. The house was acquired in 1924 by the Dickens Fellowship and transformed into the treasure-house of Dickensiana which is the **Dickens House** museum.

The builder Thomas Cubitt lived in later life at **No.53**. As he moved out, J M Levy, founder of the Daily Telegraph, moved in to **No.51**. A blue plaque erected in 1995 at **No.58** identifies the first flat to be shared, on leaving Oxford, by the feminist authors Winifred Holtby and Vera Brittain (mother of Shirley Williams). **No.62** today serves as offices of the Fulbright Commission. Residents on the opposite side of the street have included the poet Charlotte Mew at **No.10**; James Agate, the film and drama critic, at **No.14**; and much earlier at the same address the Rev. Sydney Smith (1771-1845) 'author and wit' (Fig 9), and preacher at the Foundling Hospital chapel, as a further plaque confirms.

Continue ahead along **JOHN STREET**, one of the area's gems, with splendid doorways and a glorious variety of architectural detail, though 20th-century intrusions slightly mar the overall effect. The upper west side had been built by 1760, but the rest of the street was completed only some 40 years later. In the Victorian period its fine 'first rate' houses, built for affluent Georgian families, were converted into offices for charities and trade associations; for solicitors, accountants, quantity surveyors, and the occasional publisher. North of Roger

9   *Witty Rev Sydney Smith in serious pose, c.1840.*

Street, arched doorways with imposing outsize doors with semicircular fanlights, and railings with urned finials, are the order of the day. A recent arrival at **No.15** is the Chartered Institute of Water & Environmental Management, whose centenary in 1995 is celebrated by a plaque. A large (working) clock hangs outside **No.11**, still inscribed 'Royal Oak' after the benefit society of that name, based here until the early 1980s. **No.10** housed Holborn's first public library, opened in 1891. The houses opposite at **Nos.22-28** are notable for the rectangular fanlights. On the corner of Roger Street, at **No.21**, the offices of **Meed House** date from 1938, sporting the easily missed figures of two female nudes. **No.21a** next door, built after WW II in inappropriate plain red brick, and now occupied by Cable & Wireless (*see also* pp 15,17), stands on the site of John Street Baptist Chapel, which opened in 1818 and flourished here until ravaged by enemy action in WW II.

South of the King's Arms, the east side of the street is a mixture of original and rebuilt houses, where porticoes with broken pediments predominate. Here congregated a number of missionary societies, including the Open Air Mission founded in 1853 and still at **No.19**; while until the 1950s the Africa Inland Mission occupied **No.3**. Rebuilt **No.6** stands on the site of one home, reputedly, of the

10   *Isaac D'Israeli at 22 Theobalds Road, where his son Benjamin Disraeli was born; Isaac subsequently moved to Bloomsbury Square.*

D'Israeli family (see later). 20th-century **No.1** is a former branch of the Westminster Bank, now converted into flats. Meanwhile, on the opposite side, **No.30** was home, in 1847-58, to the Ladies' Charity School, founded in St Sepulchre's in 1702, with royal patronage, and later removed to Queen Square (p 25). **Nos.31-32**, rebuilt in facsimile, were headquarters from 1914 of the Shaftesbury Society & Ragged School Union. A bust and plaque honour John Kirk, 'Christian philanthropist and friend of children', and a mainstay of the charity for many years. After its departure for SW1 c.1960, the Metropolitan Water Board (later Thames Water) moved in, appropriately in view of the district's water supply associations; a newspaper group is now in occupation. **Nos.34-36**, with especially fine Ionic porticoes, date from 1760, while **No.33** is a modern reconstruction. The Law Commission overlook Gray's Inn gardens from **Conquest House**, a 1950s red-brick block.

Arriving again at **THEOBALDS ROAD**, glance to the right where **Holborn Library** was opened in 1959 as a central library for the former borough, and much acclaimed at the time. It now embraces Camden Local Studies and Archives Centre, whose excellent resources (documentary and human) have been indispensable to the authors of this book and its sister volumes. Turn left, passing at

**Nos.12-22** a short but imposing Georgian terrace, built c.1770, with fine doorways, and railings topped by torch flambé finials. These houses survived the 1878 road widening, for unlike Theobalds Row to the west, this end of the King's Road had been spared the earlier depredations of Barbon and his contemporaries, had remained of a generous width, and scarcely needed widening. At **No.22**, a plaque commemorates the birth in 1804 of future prime minister Benjamin Disraeli here at the home of his father Isaac D'Israeli (Fig 10), a man of letters whose routine included a daily stroll to the British Museum. The smart Corinthian doorway at **No.6** beyond once gave access to a teashop of the ubiquitous J. Lyons chain. At the junction with Gray's Inn Road is the **Yorkshire Grey** pub (rebuilt 1877), its equine name perhaps influenced by the cavalry barracks which once stood in Gray's Inn Lane. Over the main door is a gilded horse's head, while high above in the gable is a colourful effigy of a mounted cavalryman, visible from the opposite corner, where stands the now empty old Holborn police station of 1896.

Turn south along the lower reaches of Gray's Inn Road to return to Chancery Lane Underground station (closed Sundays); or make use of one of the several local bus routes.

## Route 5
# Around Coram's Fields

Captain Thomas Coram, a shipwright and master mariner, settled in Rotherhithe c.1720 after nearly 30 years in New England. Appalled by the regular sight of infants abandoned to die in London streets by their hapless mothers, he campaigned for 17 years for the establishment of an institution to protect them. Twenty-one 'Ladies of Nobility and Distinction' were eventually persuaded to petition George II, and the **Foundling Hospital** (FH) was established by Royal Charter in 1739, opening in cramped accommodation in Hatton Garden. Two years later Coram's 'ladies', and some gentlemen, bought from the 6th Earl of Salisbury a 56-acre field called Conditeschotte north of Lamb's Conduit. Because the Earl refused to sell less than the whole of the field, the FH had land surplus to requirements. The 'hospital' (really more of an orphanage) was built near the middle of the property, on the site of present Coram's Fields, leaving undeveloped meadow land on either side and to the north (Fig 11, and cover).

In 1756 the FH received a parliamentary grant, but this was withdrawn 4 years later, leaving the institution in parlous financial state, and by 1790 it was forced to consider developing its spare land for housing. Though keen to raise income, the governors were anxious to preserve 'the

---

### Street names along route 5 and their origin

**Brunswick**
Caroline of Brunswick,
wife of Prince Regent
**Grenville**
Lord Grenville, Foreign Secretary 1791-1801
**Guilford**
Lord North, Duke of Guil(d)ford,
president of Foundling Hospital (FH) (d1792)
**Heathcote**
Michael, FH governor from 1810
**Lansdowne**
William Petty, Marquis of Lansdowne,
Prime Minister 1782-83
**Mecklenburg**
Queen Charlotte was daughter
of Grand Duke of Mecklenburg-Strelitz

---

advantages of its present open situation' for their young charges, and to ensure a development that would 'rather raise than depress the Character of this Hospital itself as an Object of National Munificence'. Leafy Brunswick and Mecklenburgh Squares, flanking the FH site, and each with houses on only three sides, reflect this

aspiration. Plots were let to a number of speculative builders, pre-eminent among them the young Scot James Burton, a favourite of John Nash, who was also active on the Duke of Bedford's estate to the west. By 1802 he had built 586 houses on the Foundling estate. The architect Samuel Pepys Cockerell was appointed as surveyor.

This walk covers the eastern half of the Foundling estate, although we start in the west. Turn left on leaving Russell Square Underground station, then left again along Herbrand Street to reach **GUILFORD STREET**; cross this and follow it eastward on its south side. Laid out in 1792, it was built mainly by Burton in the following 5 years, many houses having chimneypots made at nearby Bagnigge Wells (p 57). A terrace of Georgian houses lines the north side at **Nos.61-81**, some with original façades, some, such as Doric-pilastered **Nos.70-73**, rebuilt after wartime damage; of **No.74** only the ground floor remains. Travel writer George A Sala (*see also* p 47) lived at **No.64** in 1864-6, Sydney Smith at **No.77** in 1803. Notice the off-white band running between ground and first floors of some houses. Cockerell planned the street to comprise 'first-rate' houses at the west end, reducing progressively to 'fourth-rate' further east. The 'stone string' was to run continuously along the whole length of the street to disguise the gradual degradation in quality, an effect wholly lost in 20th-century redevelopment. No.82, at the

junction with Grenville Street, is still a bomb-site 50 years after the end of hostilities, of which the Guilford Arms pub on the opposite corner was also a victim.

The south side of the street is almost wholly modern. At the corner with Russell Square we have the 8-storey **President Hotel**, on the site of Bolton House, successively home in the 18th century to Lord Baltimore, the Duke of Bolton, and Lord Loughborough. The pathway leading into Queen Square has in recent decades assumed the name **Queen Anne's Walk**, although there is no sign to that effect. Next come the flats of **Guilford Court** and Queen Court, on the site of No.54, home in 1852-61 to architect Matthew Digby Wyatt (*see also* p 51). Beside a second footway into Queen Square is the 10-storey block of the **Institute of Neurology** (1970-78), the sickly brutalism of its exterior scarcely conducive to nervous composure! It covers the site of Queen Square House, a substantial mansion of 1779 with a large projecting portico facing west (Fig 3, p 23). It could have been here that George III was rumoured to have stayed (p 26) 'in a ground floor room overlooking Guildford Street'. The house was bought by the National Hospital in 1953, and

*11   The Foundling Hospital, c.1830, with the chapel in the centre, boys' and girls' wings to left and right.*

subsequently demolished in spite of a preservation order, the discovery that its porch had been rebuilt in 1830 having supposedly weakened the case against its destruction. In 1864-99 it served as a Presbyterian theological college (previously at No.29 Queen Square). It subsequently housed Jews' College until 1932, when it was converted into flats 'for ladies'.

Next along Guilford Street, and adorned by a frieze depicting the nine Muses, is the **Princess Royal Nurses' Home**, designed for the neighbouring children's hospital by Stanley Hall, and improbable winner of the RIBA London Medal in 1936. Church architect William M Teulon lived on the site at No.42 in 1854-67. The modern block of the University's (Nuffield) **Institute of Child Health** covers the site of No.25, home in 1879-90 to Algernon Charles Swinburne. Another poet living in the street was the Scot Edwin Muir, who settled here with his novelist wife Willa Anderson in 1919.

Yet another poet, the 'decadent' Ernest C Dowson, a friend of Yeats, lived in **GUILFORD PLACE**, the northern egress from Lamb's Conduit Street. Cockerell had a crescent in mind when he planned the Place, as the shape of the roadway suggests, but builders balked at the cost of building it, and William Harrison, who undertook the task in 1793, substituted a square-cut shape, as evidenced by the old houses remaining at

**Nos.3-6** on the east side. Here in the 18th century stood the Coach & Horses tavern, where on dark winter evenings in 1756 an armed escort could be hired by pedestrians wishing to walk north through the dangerous fields to the Bull at Kentish Town. The central traffic island contains a closed Victorian underground lavatory, and the long-disused Francis Whiting Fountain, adorned by the 1870 statue (Fig 12; sculptor unknown) of a kneeling girl pouring water from a jug, a clear allusion to neighbouring Lamb's Conduit. Guilford Street was built on the very banks of the Fleet tributary which fed it, and the New River Company was initially unwilling to lay on a water supply to the street, claiming that the ground was too soft for its pipes.

On your left are **Coram's Fields**, on the site of the Foundling Hospital. This closed in 1926, since central London was no longer considered a good environment for children. Most of the buildings were demolished, and the land sold, the proceeds being used to build a large boarding school at Berkhamsted. Today we can only imagine the grand buildings which once stood in the middle distance, beyond the striking green-roofed 20th-century 'pavilion' (shelter). Designed by Theodore Jacobsen, a founding governor of the FH, the buildings opened in 1745. In the centre was the chapel, which soon became a highly fashionable place to worship, the novel institution having excited much interest and curiosity among the upper classes. The composer Handel, another founding governor, raised large amounts of money for the FH through benefit performances, including the première in England of *Messiah*. East and west wings housed respectively girls and boys: the sexes were always segregated, except on Christmas Day.

Stay on the south side of Guilford Street to view the Foundling Hospital's lodges, two of the few structures that escaped demolition in 1926. In a niche here, it is said, mothers once left their babies in a basket, before ringing a bell and departing. Desperate mothers came from all over the country to seek admission for their offspring, and the hospital was unable to cope. FH admission policies varied greatly over time. For a while there was a balloting system, whereby the acceptance or rejection of an infant was determined by the drawing of a white or a black ball. Infant foundlings were farmed out to an army of foster parents all over England until the age of 4, when they returned to the FH until their early teens. The regime was spartan, but remarkably humane by the standards of the day. Children were always treated as individuals, each receiving a name, often of a FH governor or his wife, or of a character from history or literature. Girls, on leaving, usually entered domestic service, while boys became apprentices or joined the armed

services. The FH aimed to give them an education befitting their lowly status in life. Of the two colonnades surviving on either side of the playground, that on the west side was at one time used by the boys for making rope, which was sold for use by the fishing fleet. Since 1977 it has housed the animals of a flourishing 'city farm'.

When the FH closed, most of its land was sold to a property speculator named James White, whose plan was to relocate Covent Garden market onto the Hospital site, and to transform nearby streets into an industrial estate, a proposal mercifully scotched by a huge local outcry. A fund-raising campaign to turn the site into a children's playground reached its target with generous help from Harold Harmsworth (Lord Rothermere), as stated on a plaque in a niche facing Guilford Street. Opened in 1936 as the Harmsworth Memorial Playground, and claiming with justification to be 'the world's finest', it now serves local children from numerous cultural backgrounds. Please note the unusual, but prudent, rule that adults are admitted only if accompanied by a child!

(For the headquarters of the Thomas Coram Foundation, the charity continuing the work of the Foundling Hospital, *see* p 47.)

Continue east along Guilford Street, passing a very plain and unimaginative 1960s London University block on your right, which covers the site of a house immortalised by Thackeray in his

*Ballad of Eliza Davis*:
  In this street there lived a housemaid,
  If you particularly ask me where —
  Vy, it was at four and twenty
  Guildford Street by Brunswick Square.
At the eastern end of the street, some late-18th-century houses survive, with Cockerell's white stone string again in evidence. By Edwardian times, most had become boarding houses, small hotels, or offices. **No.10** was then the headquarters of the Rational Dress League, a group advocating practical clothing for (especially) women. It now belongs to the Sick Children's Trust, a 'home from home' for parents of patients at the Hospital for Sick Children nearby. This was opened in 1990 by Sarah, Duchess of York, according to the plaque. Another plaque, at **No.6**, recalls an earlier St Nicholas's Nursery, associated with the same hospital.

Cross to the north side, and return westward past attractive **London House**, a hall of residence originally for male overseas students (now only graduates), with entrance in Mecklenburgh Square. F C Goodenough (d.1934), chairman of Barclay's Bank, was the driving force behind its promoters, the Dominion Students' Hall Trust. The southern block, its ground floor faced with knapped flint, was designed by Sir Herbert Baker (1862-1946), and opened by Queen Mary in 1937. A stone plaque on the south wall records the dedication of the house library to engineer Sir Charles Parsons (1854-1931), perfecter of the compound steam turbine.

West of London House, turn right into short **MECKLENBURGH PLACE**, known until 1938 as Caroline Place. On the Ordnance Survey map of 1936, it appeared disarmingly as Sally Place, a name strangely absent from other contemporary sources, perhaps because the name, with its topical Gracie Fields connections, was considered too plebeian for its princely surroundings.

Almost at once we are in peaceful **MECKLENBURGH SQUARE**, possibly our area's best-kept secret. Actress Flora Robson lived in 1936-7 at No.6 in the south-east corner, where war-torn houses later gave way to an extension of London House on your right, built by the London Goodenough Trust in 1961. The houses and gardens of the square (c.1810) were designed by Joseph Kay, a pupil of Cockerell, who had by then resigned his surveyorship in a huff, having been accused of failing to enforce standards: not all the builders active on the estate were as scrupulous as Burton. Cockerell now magnanimously supervised Kay's work here as an unpaid consultant.

The east side of the square (*see* frontispiece) was based loosely on Robert Adam's work in Fitzroy Square, its magnificent façade intended to attract the right kind of resident to this less favourable end of 'Bloomsbury'. It is only partially stuccoed — fine rendered sections, adorned with wreaths and festoons, alternating with plain brick — probably for effect rather than economy. So pleased were the FH governors that they paid Kay eight times the fee he had requested. In the 1930s the London Welsh Association was at **No.11**, backing onto what is now the London Welsh Centre in Gray's Inn Road (p 62). The Welsh language was often to be heard in the Portland Arms, a long demolished pub on the corner of nearby Millman Street. So, at least, reported Graham Greene, who in 1938 rented a studio in the square where, high on benzedrine, he worked on *The Confidential Agent* every morning and *The Power and the Glory* in the afternoon. **No.18** was home to the illustrator Marjorie Quennell, and later to poet laureate John Masefield. Two blue plaques on **No.21** refer to Sir Syed Ahmed Khan (1817-98), Muslim reformer and scholar, resident in this house 1869-70 (having served in the Indian Civil Service, he had come to England to secure a Western education for his two sons) and to R H Tawney, the Socialist historian, who lived there in 1951. **Nos.21-25**, forming the stuccoed centrepiece of the east side of the square,

*12  The Francis Whiting Fountain and Water-Bearer statue in Guilford Place before WW II.*

have fine Ionic columns. The West Central Collegiate School, one of the longest surviving dame schools (of the better class) was at **No.25** from 1858 to 1915. The flats of war-damaged Byron Court (Nos.26-34) were rebuilt as a fair facsimile, though now with a single entrance at **No.26**, and disappointingly modern dormer windows. No.29 housed Tancred Borenius, the Finnish art historian and diplomat.

Leading from the north-east corner of the square is short **MECKLENBURGH STREET**, where on the east side **Nos.1-8**, with a continuous row of iron balconies, miraculously survived WW II.

**HEATHCOTE STREET**, beyond, was virtually flattened, **Nos.1-5** on the north side being a modern neo-Georgian pastiche. One old street sign in the short eastern stretch of the road did survive: 'leading to ... Caroline Place', it announces, anachronistically. Set in the pavement nearby is a plate marking the Foundling estate boundary. A bar gate here once protected the good folk of Mecklenburgh Square from unwelcome intrusions, but today the only gates are the very ornate ones guarding the entrance to St George's Gardens (p 51) at the west end of the cul-de-sac. Bollards still prevent cars from entering the square from the north-east, thereby contributing substantially to its peaceful air.

Return to the north-east corner of **MECKLENBURGH SQUARE**, where **William Goodenough House**, the female counterpart of London House, was run by the 'Sister Trust' until it merged with the male establishment in 1965. A plaque records its erection 8 years earlier, aided by the Lord Mayor's National Thanksgiving Fund. On this site were No.35a, home of actress Fay Compton in 1933-35, and No.37, sometime headquarters of the Hogarth Press: Virginia and Leonard Woolf moved here in 1939 to escape the noise of building work in Tavistock Square, only to be bombed out the following year while away at their country retreat at Rodmell, Sussex. The scene of

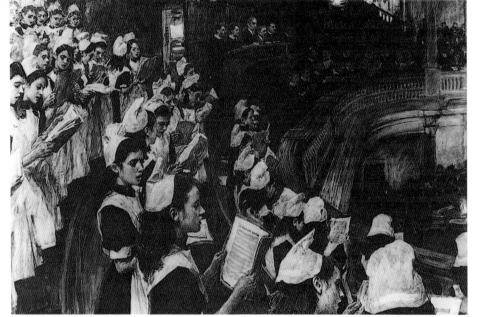

*13*
*P'haps you know the Fondling Chapel,*
*Where the little children sings?*
*Lord! I like to hear, on Sundays,*
*Them there pretty little things.*
　　*The Ballad of Eliza Davis (Thackeray)*

devastation greeting them on their return is vividly described in Virginia's diary.

Surviving houses on this secluded north side of the square include **No.38**, home in 1906-11 of artists Sir William Nicholson and his better-known son Ben; and **No.43**, residence in 1857-60 of Sir William Cubitt, civil engineer, Lord Mayor of London, and surviving brother of the builder Thomas. **No.44** was home to a strange household in 1917, when D H and Frieda Lawrence were guests of Dorothy Yorke, mistress of writer Richard Aldington, then away on active service. Aldington's wife, Hilda Doolittle (the American imagist poet 'HD'), was meanwhile elsewhere in the house, recovering from a miscarriage. It is poetic justice, perhaps, that Hilda is the one commemorated by an unofficial blue plaque. After WW I Dorothy L Sayers moved in, and here created Lord Peter Wimsey, investing the fruits of her success in No.24 Great James Street (p 37). Later residents at No.44 were R H Tawney, in 1922, and, much later, former local MP Lena Jeger. **No.46** was the home in 1878-84 of the journalist and novelist George A Sala, his neighbour at **No.47** being the traveller Lewis Wingfield.

From the north-west corner of the square, follow a permissive but littered footpath westward, passing (on the left) the **Wolfson Centre** of the Institute of Child Health. The Coram's Fields football pitch south of the path marks roughly the site of the main blocks of the Foundling Hospital. In the central block, the chapel, daily services were held for 'Thomas Coram's children', dressed in a characteristic uniform (Fig 13), right up until WW I.

We emerge into the north side of **BRUNSWICK SQUARE**, beside a statue of Thomas Coram (by William MacMillan, 1963) in front of **No.40**, headquarters of the **Thomas Coram Foundation**, which continues Coram's legacy in the provision of adoption services and counselling for young people leaving care. Designed by J M Sheppard, the 1937 building was erected on land retained when the rest of the FH site was sold. A bust of the Captain surmounts the entrance, while the Court Room inside is an exact replica of that in the old FH, incorporating the original rococo plasterwork on walls and ceiling. The many paintings lining the walls include William Hogarth's satirical *March of the Guards to Finchley*, and his magnificent portrait of Coram, from which the 1963 statue outside is derived. Hogarth, a founding governor, persuaded many notable artists to donate their work to the FH, which became, in effect, London's first public art gallery. (NB at the time of writing, the Foundation is not open to the public except by appointment.) In 1998 the site to the east, once the FH garden, was being redeveloped by the Foundation as a new Children's Centre.

Brunswick Square was developed earlier than its easterly neighbour, but of the relatively plain houses built here by Burton in 1795-1802, not one survives. Though never fashionable, the square was always respectable: Macaulay referred to 'the quiet folk' who lived there. It is praised in Jane Austen's *Emma*, where Emma's married sister Isabella proclaims that 'our part of London is so very superior to most others ... we are so very airy'. The poet Bryan Waller Procter (p 13) lived in the square in his youth. Today, the red-brick bulk of the University's **School of Pharmacy**, founded in 1842, dominates most of the north side. Its new building here, by Herbert J Rowse, was begun in 1939, but not fully occupied for over 30 years. Nos.32 and 34, on the site, were successively home in 1803-16 to John Hunter, a physician and FH vice-president, not to be confused with a namesake, the royal surgeon and anatomist who gave his name to nearby Hunter Street. John Leech, the caricaturist, illustrator of Dickens, and friend of Thackeray, lived at No.32 in 1854-62. Five 'Bloomsberries' lived at No.38 in 1911: Virginia and Adrian Stephen shared the house with John Maynard Keynes, Duncan Grant and Leonard Woolf until the following year, when Virginia and Leonard married and left. The novelist E M Forster, a friend of the Woolfs, lived in 1929-39 at No.26 on the west side of the square, now wholly replaced by the shops and flats of the Brunswick Centre (p 53). Unlike the private gardens of Mecklenburgh Square, those here are public. Walk through them to the south side, where houses have given way to **International Hall** (1962), a London University student hostel, whose ground-floor walls are enlivened by the badges of 21 (sometime) Commonwealth countries, with the curious addition of Austria.

East of the Hall is short **LANSDOWNE TERRACE**, built c.1792, where Burton's **Nos.1-4** survive. Opposite is part of the FH's western colonnade, and a strip of grass where city farm sheep sometimes safely graze. Retrace your steps and turn left at the roundabout into parallel **GRENVILLE STREET**. On its west side are the flats of **Downing Court**, and the Café Romano at **No.11**, which was the Foundling estate office until the 1970s. Nos.8-10, still a bombsite, were once a nurses' home of the ENT hospital in Gray's Inn Road (p 67).

An archway, surmounted by a carved inscription, leads into cobbled **COLONNADE**, along which we turn. Determined to preserve the district's residential character, the FH governors allowed commercial development only in this south-west corner of the estate. While the south side consisted of stables, now predictably garages and workshops, these faced onto a colonnaded shopping parade.

Above one shop were assembly rooms, where Dr Roget (p 54) sometimes lectured. By the 1870s the small Georgian shops had become a slum, and were demolished, leaving only the present brick wall. Halfway along on the left, a Victorian taking-in door and gantry survive at **Nos.19-23**. Nearer the ground (and sometimes obscured by parked cars) are reminders of the boundary of St Pancras with St George's Bloomsbury: the parts of the Foundling estate within the latter parish are covered in the next walk (Route 6). Almost opposite, still set in the cobbles, is a tiny metal plate, inscribed 'NR', and probably put there by the New River Company which had been so reluctant to bring water here in the first place. At the west end of the Colonnade is the Contemporary Wardrobe Collection (pop'n'rock costumiers), on whose outside wall is the mysterious painted legend 'Horse Hospital'. One possible clue to its meaning is that a vet named Charles Smith practised at No.43 Colonnade a century ago, when the mews was very much a preserve of horsecab proprietors. Turn right, past the old **Friend at Hand** pub, and right again to return to our starting point at Russell Square Underground station; or proceed to route 6.

# East & West of Marchmont Street

Most of the area covered by this circular walk lay in the parish of St George's Bloomsbury, and thus in the later borough of Holborn. Tavistock Place was the northern boundary both of the latter and of the Foundling estate, on whose land most of the streets were built, many having names recalling benefactors of the Foundling Hospital (FH).

Leaving Russell Square Underground station behind you, cross the road (Bernard Street) safely and proceed north along Marchmont Street. Ignoring for the moment the ziggurat steps of the Brunswick Centre, turn left into **CORAM STREET**. Dating from 1800-04, and originally Great Coram Street, this continued eastwards to Brunswick Square before the Brunswick Centre (p 53) was built 1969-72; its present-day rump is entirely 20th-century. The **Forte Posthouse** (formerly Bloomsbury Crest Hotel), built by McAlpine back-to-back with the firm's headquarters, stands on the site of No.6, home in 1860-62 of early feminist Emily Faithfull, founder of the Victoria Press. Here too was No.13, the

## Street names along route 6 and their origin

**Bernard**
Sir Thomas, FH vice-president 1806

**Compton**
Samuel Compton Cox, FH treasurer 1806

**Coram**
'Captain' Thomas, father of the Foundling Hospital (FH)

**Handel**
George Friederic, composer, FH organist and benefactor

**Henrietta**
Wife of Sir Stephen Gaselee (d.1838), FH vice-president

**Herbrand**
Herbrand Arthur Russell, 11th Duke of Bedford, 1st Mayor of St Pancras

**Hunter**
John (d.1793), anatomist and royal surgeon

**Kenton**
Benjamin (1719-1800), vintner and FH benefactor

**Marchmont**
Hugh Hume (1708-94), Earl of Marchmont, FH governor

**Tavistock**
Marquess of Tavistock, title of the heirs to the Bedford dukedom

**Wakefield**
The Pindar of Wakefield tavern (p 79) stood in Gray's Inn Road

house, in 1837-43, of William Makepeace Thackeray, then struggling to establish himself as a writer. His wife Isabella had a mental breakdown when their third child was born, and had to be entrusted to a Paris sanatorium. In his *Vanity Fair*, Mr Todd lives in Great Coram Street. Thackeray shared the house in 1837 with the caricaturist John Leech (p 29), and 5 years later with Edward Fitzgerald, the translator of Omar Khayyam's *Rubaiyat*. At the west end of Coram Street, 1930s **Witley Court** flats occupy the site of the Russell Institution. Built by James Burton in 1802 as assembly rooms, it burned down the next year, and was rebuilt as

a literary and scientific club (Fig 14), whose library eventually held 16,000 books. Thackeray and Leech were members, as was Charles Dickens.

A colossal modern concrete tower, part of the adjacent McAlpine complex, stands at the corner of **HERBRAND STREET**. Here turn right, but not before looking down its southern end which, as Little Guilford Street, once housed the National School of Christ Church (Woburn Square). On the west side is the white

*14  The Russell Institution, Coram Street in the 19th century. Witley Court (1930s) now covers the site.*

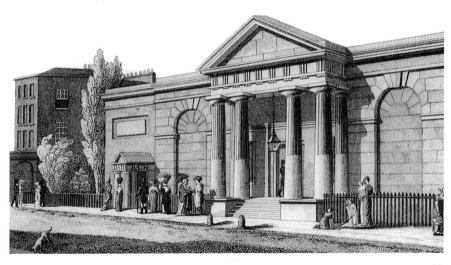

**London Taxi Centre**, a multi-level garage built for the Daimler Hire Co. in 1931, and designed in Art Deco style by Wallis, Gilbert & Partners, architects of the Hoover factory. Herbrand Street forms the eastern boundary of the Bedford estate, and was re-named in 1901 when the 11th Duke was mayor of the new Borough of Holborn. Its northern reaches, when named Little Coram Street, were much narrower, and accessed through an archway at the north end. The west side is occupied today by **Coram House**, **Thackeray House** and **Dickens House**, three red-brick blocks of municipal housing separated by lawns, erected by Holborn Borough Council on land bought from the duke in 1898, and replacing the mean courts of Abbey Place and Tavistock Mews. These contrast with **Peabody Buildings** opposite, eight blocks in stock brick built around a courtyard in 1884, after slum clearance by the Metropolitan Board of Works. Financed through the generosity of the American George Peabody, who bequeathed £¹/₂ million to rehouse London's 'respectable poor', they are still administered by the Peabody Trust. They are recognisably the model for Brown's Buildings, home of the heroine in *Marcella*, the 1894 novel by Russell Square resident Mrs Humphry Ward (Fig 15).

Passing the diminutive Bloomsbury ambulance station, emerge into **TAVISTOCK PLACE**, where across the

15 *Mary (Mrs Humphry) Ward, photographed c.1898.*

street and a little to the west is **Mary Ward House**. In 1890 Mrs Ward opened a social centre at University Hall in Gordon Square, followed a year later by clubs for men and boys at Marchmont Hall. Newspaper owner John Passmore Edwards was persuaded to finance a new building in Tavistock Place for a 'settlement', providing ordinary people with educational and social amenities

normally available only to the rich. An architectural competition judged by Norman Shaw was won by two University Hall residents, A Dunbar Smith and Cecil Brewer. Their creation, opened in 1897 as the Passmore Edwards Settlement, with a library and large hall, has been hailed as a triumph of Arts & Crafts design, the plain exterior belying the treasures within. Within a year Mrs Ward had opened the country's first play centre, and the first school for disabled children. The latter moved into its own building (next door) in 1906, becoming the LCC School for the Physically Defective, and remaining a special school until 1961. Its old gate may be seen on the right. Mrs Ward died in 1920, and a year later the centre was re-named, after her, the Mary Ward Settlement, under which name it played host in the 1930s to the Tavistock Little Theatre. In 1961 the freehold was bought by the Nuffield Trust, and the buildings were restored for occupation by the National Institute for Social Work. The boys' club migrated to Coram's Fields, while other settlement activities moved into the school building next door (now occupied by the Learning Agency) pending a permanent move to Queen Square (p 23).

On the site west of Mary Ward House once stood No.37, a large villa occupied 1826-44 by the physicist Francis Baily, who here conducted experiments to 'weigh the earth' or, more accurately, to determine its density. A detached house, set back from the road, was essential to avoid interference from vibrations. The house was later occupied by Matthew Digby Wyatt, the architect responsible for the decorative work at Paddington Station. The western extremity of Tavistock Place lay on the Bedford estate, hence the Russell-related name. Building was begun here c.1805 by James Burton, but **Nos.2-14**, on the south side, are a recent neo-Georgian pastiche. The antiquarian John Britton lived at No.10 (then No.2) in 1811-20; followed later (1835-37) by Zachary Macaulay, an opponent of slavery, and father of Thomas Babington Macaulay. No.16 (then No.9) was home in 1810-11 to James Elmes, architect, antiquary, and compiler of *Metropolitan Improvements*.

Walk east along either pavement, passing on the south side a continuous range of early houses at **Nos.18-44**, many of them converted into hotels. On the opposite side, by contrast, nothing original remains. East of Mary Ward House stood No.34, once home to Mrs Mary Ann Clark, a mistress of the ('grand old') Duke of York, second son of George III. The novelist John Galt lived at No.32 in 1815-23; and No.33 was where Jerome K Jerome 'chummed' in 1889 with George Wingrave, the model for George in *Three Men in a Boat*. On the site is early 20th-century **No.13**, now flats, but occupied

during WW II by RAF Coastal Command. Immediately adjacent stood the proprietary Woburn (or St Andrew's) Chapel (1803), a neo-Gothic blend of brick and stucco, and described as 'one of the first pretended revivals in this town of our Ancient Architecture'. Its extremely High-Church practices often landed it in trouble with the bishop; disused by 1892, it was demolished in 1900. Beyond the former headquarters of Express Dairies, now housing the **British Transport Police**, Marchmont Street intersects.

Continue along the eastern end of Tavistock Place, originally Cox Street, then Compton Street, before it merged with the western half, radically renumbered, in 1938. (Samuel Compton Cox was a treasurer of the FH.) The north side here was built on a narrow strip of land belonging to Charles Fitzroy, Baron Southampton, a detached fragment of a large estate whose main part stretched north from Fitzrovia to Highgate.

An archway leads through into sunken, cobbled, **COMPTON PLACE**, which preserves the old name of its parent street. In Victorian times it housed a receiving station, mission hall and ragged school; today it is the entrance to the privately-run youth hostel known as the 'Generator' (p 71).

Proceeding beyond the Judd Street traffic lights, turn right along **WAKEFIELD STREET**, victim of a V2 attack in 1944. Off the east side, in what

was once Regent Square Mews, is a dairyman's yard, now used by Express Dairies, which in the 19th century served the milk contractors Freeth & Pocock. To the right, facing Handel Street, once stood the Henrietta Street Chapel, a Baptist establishment (Fig 16, p 52) which flourished here from 1822 to 1909. It later became the Regent's Working Men's Club, and was known before WW II as the Regent Square Institute. The old brick building to the left of the yard entrance was the lecture hall of the original Scotch Church (p 81) which it adjoined.

Gates lead into attractive **St George's Gardens**, originally two burial grounds. They occupied parallel plots, acquired by the Church in 1715 on the very edge of town, to serve what were soon to become the two parishes of St George the Martyr (1723) and St George's Bloomsbury (1731). Among those buried here were Anna Cromwell, Oliver's sixth and favourite daughter, and several notables whom we have encountered elsewhere such as William Brockedon, Zachary Macaulay and Robert Nelson, the first person to be buried here, hence the plot's original popular name of Nelson's Burial Ground. Also interred here were the headless bodies of twelve Jacobites, hanged, drawn and quartered in 1746; and here occurred a very early recorded case of grave-robbing. In 1777 two resurrectionists, one of them a gravedigger, were sentenced to 6 months' imprisonment, and a whipping at the cart's tail from Kingsgate Street to Seven Dials, a traditional route for such spectacles. The site was laid out as public gardens in 1884-5, with the customary drinking fountain. Although some of the gravestones and table-tombs survive, their inscriptions are largely illegible. The terracotta statue of Euterpe, muse of instrumental music, was salvaged from the demolished Apollo & the Muses pub in Tottenham Court Road.

Return to Wakefield Street, at whose southern end diagonal marks carved in the kerbstones record the north-eastern extremity of the eccentrically shaped parish of St George's Bloomsbury.

**HENRIETTA MEWS**, a tiny access road, leads off the right-angled junction with **HANDEL STREET**, formerly Henrietta Street. The street was re-named after the composer, a generous benefactor of the FH, whose donations included a copy of the score of his *Messiah*, and an organ for its chapel (now in St Andrew Holborn). The Italian patriot Ugo Foscolo (1778-1827), died in extreme poverty at long-demolished No.19. Original houses, partly refaced, remain on the south-east side at **Nos.4-7**.

Handel Street is bisected by busy **HUNTER STREET**, built on the line of an old track running north from Lamb's Conduit. No.54, at its south end, was the birthplace of author and art critic, John Ruskin. As a small boy he loved watching water-carts being filled from a stand-pipe outside, through 'beautiful little trap doors and pipes like boa-constrictors'. The house, which had borne a brown plaque, was swept away to make way for the Brunswick Centre. Only two early houses do survive, on the east side at **Nos.3-4**. Another nearby is said to have been the sometime residence of Mrs Fitzherbert, the Catholic widow married secretly and illegally to the Prince of Wales (later George IV) in 1785. On the site today is the former Royal Free Hospital Medical School for Women, a pioneering establishment opened in 1874 by Mrs Elizabeth Garrett Anderson. Restored by Avanti in 1988, and now serving as a **health centre**, the building has an imposing portico with a broken pediment. Many of its details are imitated in **Jenner House**, a neighbouring residential block.

Carefully cross Hunter Street, and

*16  The Henrietta (Baptist) Chapel, from an 1859 watercolour.*

continue along the western half of Handel Street, passing on the right the former (c.1908) **drill hall** of the 1st (City of London Battalion), the London Regiment, previously based in Fitzroy Square and earlier still in Queen Square. Still used for Territorial Army purposes, the building rounds the corner, as do we, into the rump of **KENTON STREET**. Benjamin Kenton, a tavern waiter turned vintner, made a fortune by inventing a means of bottling ale so that it could be shipped to seamen in hot climates without the cork popping out. He left his money to charity, the FH being among the beneficiaries. His eponymous street would no longer exist if plans to continue the Brunswick Centre northwards had not been frustrated by lack of finance. Refurbished **Aberdeen Mansions** and **Robsart Mansions** are all that remain of a row of six mansion flat blocks, c.1900, mostly named after works of Sir Walter Scott (*Ivanhoe*, *Kenilworth*). Comic magician Tommy Cooper lived in Waverley House in 1952-55. The Victorian survival at **Nos.73-75** was once a printer's.

Briefly retrace your earlier steps west along Tavistock Place to the traffic lights, and turn right to inspect the north end of **MARCHMONT STREET**. Originating in the early 1790s, this was at first largely middle-class residential. Watercolourists John Skinner Prout and William Henry Hunt both lived here before 1840, by which time the street was developing into a typical Victorian local 'high street'. Some shops thrived here for generations. The fishmonger's business of Samuel Gordon on the north-east corner of the crossing with Tavistock Place closed in 1997 after 120 years of trading. Balfour's, a long-established bakery diagonally opposite, was an earlier casualty of rising costs and diminishing custom, and is now a pasta restaurant. The prominent inscription 'est.1826' on the north-west corner of this crossing probably relates to the business of Thomas Willis, a tea merchant who opened a branch here in the 1890s.

In 1877-78 Marchmont Street swallowed up Everett Street to the south, was renumbered and substantially rebuilt. On the west side at the north end is the site of old No.26, where Percy Bysshe Shelley, wife Mary, and stepsister-in-law Claire Clairmont stayed in 1816 before visiting Byron in Geneva. An archway, still labelled 'South Crescent Mews', once led into the old stabling area for Burton Crescent (now Cartwright Gardens, p 73), covered long ago by an Express Dairies depot. The **Lord John Russell** pub honours (according to its sign) the third son of the 6th Duke of Bedford, prime minister in 1846-52. However, the pub's landlord in the 1850s was a Mr John Russell; was there, perhaps, something tongue-in-cheek about its naming?

Return south along the central section of Marchmont Street, surprisingly leafy in summer, where older houses survive on the west side. **Nos.69-71** carry metal plates (SGB 1817/SPP 1791) testifying both to the antiquity of the premises and to the position of the old parish boundary. Comic actor Kenneth Williams lived as a child above a hairdresser's managed by his father; the present shop, 'Shampoo', is still in the same line of business. **No.39** bears an unofficial plaque to Charles Fort, who lived here in 1820-21, and founded Forteanism, the study of 'anomalous phenomena'. The pub on the corner of Coram Street was always the Marquess of Cornwallis until fatuously renamed the **Goose & Granite** in 1997.

Almost opposite, follow an arcade eastward into the **Brunswick Centre** (1969-72), a 5-storey development of shops and flats by Marchmont Properties, a McAlpine subsidiary. Designed by Patrick Hodgkinson and acclaimed by some as 'bold and uncompromising', the development has been compared by others to everything from a gun emplacement to a nuclear power station. The flats form cantilevered terraces in two long blocks — **Foundling Court** and **O'Donnell Court** — the latter named after Dr J J O'Donnell, a philanthropic local GP of the early 20th century. Between them is an often windswept, crudely colonnaded, piazza, lined by eating places and shops. A redeeming feature, by the Brunswick Square exit, is the subterranean **Renoir** cinema, opened as the 'Bloomsbury' in 1972, and specialising in classic and foreign films. Ever controversial, the Brunswick Centre made news again in 1997, when proposals for a major redevelopment by Rugby Estates (the current freeholders) were rejected by Camden Council.

Leave the precinct at the south end and descend into **BERNARD STREET**; staying on the northern pavement, walk west. The street was built by James Burton in 1799-1820, opening into Russell Square by arrangement with the Duke of Bedford. Old houses remain on the south side, where **No.28**, all of eight bays wide, comprises Nos.26-28, knocked into one to form a hotel known in the 1930s as Mackenzie's. In 1928 No.26 was a second home of the Rev. Harold Davidson, Rector of Stiffkey (Norfolk), who spent his weekends serving his parishioners, his weekdays and nights in London 'saving fallen women'. Allegations that he was saving them for his own pleasure led to his being sensationally defrocked in 1932, after which he became a seaside sideshow attraction, and, in the Biblical role of Daniel, was eventually mauled to death by a lion. **Nos.11-25** show great variety in their balconies of different sizes and shapes. On the north side none of the original houses survive, and east of **Bernard Mansions**, all is modern. The Brunswick Centre has engulfed

erstwhile No.39, home in 1808-43 of Dr Peter Mark Roget, physician and polymath, founder of the Society for the Diffusion of Useful Knowledge, lecturer at the Russell Institution (p 49) and Secretary of the Royal Society 1827-49. Only upon retirement at the age of 70 did he embark on his well-known *Thesaurus of English Words and Phrases* (first edition 1852). **No.40** was erected by Sir Robert McAlpine Ltd, builders of the adjacent hotel and shopping centre, to serve as its own headquarters. At **No.48**, on the site, artist Roger Fry (d.1934) spent his last years with Helen, the wife of mosaicist Boris Anrep.

Opposite is **Russell Square Station**, opened in 1906 on the Great Northern, Piccadilly & Brompton Railway. Admire the recent restoration of its maroon-tiled exterior before, perhaps, venturing inside for your transport home.

Route 7
# Calthorpe Estate & Fleet Valley

This walk begins and ends at the Eastman Dental Hospital bus stop in Gray's Inn Road. South of Ampton Street, and our first port of call, is the interesting split-level garden of the **Calthorpe Project**, opened in 1984 on land saved from office development by a spirited public campaign, and cared for by local community groups (present opening times variable). Do not miss two murals depicting the site before and after its transformation.

The project's name relates to the Calthorpe estate, in the northern half of which it lies. In 1706 Richard Gough, a wool merchant, bought three fields in the old manor of Portpool, which by the later 18th century had been leased to Daniel Harrison for the excavation of brick-earth. Here, we would be in the northern part of Gough's 'Middlefield'. Richard's son married into the Calthorpe family, and his grandson George, the 3rd Baron, was largely responsible for developing the estate in the early 19th century. The Project garden occupies the site of Cubitt's yard, the local base of Thomas Cubitt, the remarkable builder who revolutionised

## Street names along route 7 and their origin

**Ampton**
Suffolk country seat of the Calthorpe family

**Calthorpe**
The Calthorpes inherited land east
of Gray's Inn Road in the 18th century

**Coley**
Henry (1633-c.1695), astrologer and almanac
compiler, of Baldwin's Gardens

**Cubitt**
Thomas, master builder (1788-1855);
brother (Sir) William, a Lord Mayor of London

**Fleet**
River (now sewer) forming
Camden's eastern boundary

**Frederick**
Forename of the 4th & 5th Barons Calthorpe

**Gough**
Richard, wool merchant, bought land
in Portpool manor, 1706

**Gray's Inn**
Inn of Court, Holborn

**King's Cross**
Road junction named after a former
monument to George IV

**Langton**
Arthur Langton Nurses' Home
(Royal Free Hospital)

**Pakenham**
Another Suffolk seat of the Calthorpes

**Phoenix**
Phoenix Brass Foundry was
destroyed in WW II

**Sage**
*cf.* Saffron Hill and Herbal Hill (Holborn)

**Seddon**
Seddon's furniture factory was
on the Royal Free Hospital site

**Wells**
Bagnigge Wells, 18th-century spa

**Wren**
Sir Christopher, architect,
sometime Bloomsbury resident

the building industry by employing a permanent skilled workforce. Opened soon after 1815, the yard here, from which much of Bloomsbury (to the west) was built, eventually expanded eastwards to Cubitt Street (p 57) and beyond. The extent of the Yard may be judged from Figure 17 (p 56). The family firm merged in Edwardian times with Bloomsbury-based builders Hannen & Holland, remaining in Gray's Inn Road until the 1960s.

Walk briefly north along Gray's Inn Road, then east down residential **FREDERICK STREET** — literally down, for we are now dropping perceptibly into the valley of the Fleet river. The street is almost intact, though **Nos.4-10** were rebuilt after destruction in 1940. Variations in style and height suggest a gradual development. The western part of the street (1823-7) was built by Thomas Cubitt, the later eastern

end (1827-39) by his brother William, the future (1860) Lord Mayor of London (p 47). Thomas' showpiece is **Nos.48-52**, which have iron canopies above unusually large first-floor windows. Thomas Carlyle stayed at **No.47** for a while. The street was originally protected from public traffic by bar gates, removed in 1893; however, though it began as a middle-class haven, by the time of Booth's poverty map (c.1889) its inhabitants were categorised as comfortable working class. Perhaps the trend has been reversed by late-20th-century gentrification.

Turn right along short **AMPTON PLACE**, whose few houses were built by William Cubitt only in 1845-7, to reach **AMPTON STREET**. Barred against through traffic, the quiet street retains most of its original houses. **Nos.18-36** and **21-39** at the west end are the earliest (Thomas Cubitt, 1819-23). In 1831 Thomas and Jane Carlyle lodged at **No.33** (then No.4) with a family of Irvingites, returning again in 1834, before moving to Chelsea (LCC brown plaque). Set in the northern pavement is a varied selection of florid coal-hole covers from several different local suppliers. **Nos.11-17**, built after 1835 by William Cubitt, have strikingly sturdy pedimented porticoes, surmounted by black scallops.

Follow the lower, pedestrianised, end of the street, which penetrates a modern

17 The 1837 anniversary banquet of the City of London Conservative Association, in a pavilion specially erected in Cubitt's Yard, Gray's Inn Road - indicating how huge the site must then have been.

development of low-rise Council housing. To your right, with historically relevant names but not worth a detour, are **FLEET SQUARE** and **WELLS SQUARE**, approached from the south by **SEDDON STREET**. **SAGE WAY**, on the left, has a herbal name reminiscent of those further south (eg Saffron Hill), but we are here a good kilometre north of the Bishop of Ely's herb garden!

Turn left into **CUBITT STREET**, which was Arthur Street until 1894. It originally continued south to Wren Street, along what is now Langton Close (p 60), until bisected by the eastward expansion of Cubitt's yard and diverted into King's Cross Road. On the east side, new private housing occupies a site which once contained a GPO depot, earlier a garage (destroyed in WW II), and very much earlier the pleasure gardens of Bagnigge Wells (see below). At the north-eastern corner of the street is the former Arthur Street Baptist Chapel (later Ampton Street Baptist Church). This was built in 1861 for an oddly peripatetic congregation which had previously worshipped in Whitechapel, Aldersgate, Moorfields and Spitalfields. They must have settled down in Arthur Street, for they were still here a century later. In 1950, the war-damaged chapel was acquired by the Field Lane Foundation, a charity with its origins in the Field Lane Ragged School, Saffron Hill. Its pioneering day centre for the elderly flourished here from 1952 to 1996.

Past the chapel, turn right along Frederick Street to emerge by the **Carpenters' Arms** into **KING'S CROSS ROAD**, along which we now proceed southward. This was long ago known as the Lower Road, since it followed the once steep-sided valley of the Fleet. The river flowed a little to the west of it, on the way south from its sources at Hampstead and Highgate to join the Thames at Blackfriars. Though once a fast-flowing stream, fed by several local springs, it had by 1850 become an open sewer, soon to be condemned to an underground existence as part of the Victorian sewerage system. The Camden-Islington boundary runs along the middle of King's Cross Road, of which only the western side concerns us here. Beyond a filling station, on the right is a terrace of early Victorian houses, where between **Nos.61** and **63** is a small stone plaque, salvaged from an old boundary wall, comprising a keystone depicting a mask, and the inscription:

S + T
THIS IS BAGNIGGE
HOVSE NEARE
THE PINDER A
WAKEFEILDE
1680

The letters have been recut, and 'ST' may have been a misreading of 'SP' (St Pancras). The 'Pinder' was the well known hostelry in the Gray's Inn Road (p 00); Bagnigge (pronounced 'Bagnij') House a 17th-century residence, named after an old local family. In 1757 land here was acquired by Thomas Hughes, a Holborn tobacconist. The story goes that, unable to grow anything in his garden, he sought advice from Dr John Bevis, a scientist and astronomer, who analysed the local water and declared it to be rich in iron, with excellent purgative properties. So was born Bagnigge Wells, among the most popular and fashionable of 18th-century spas, which Hughes opened to the public in 1759.

The gardens, which straddled the river, offered a grotto, fountain and fish pond, tea arbours and a bun house, a skittle alley and bowling green (Fig 18). In the Long Room, an organ was available for concerts. By the 1770s it was regarded by City merchants and their wives as the very height of gentility:

Bon Ton's the space 'twixt
  Saturday and Monday;
And riding in a one-horse chair
  on Sunday;
'Tis drinking tea on summer
  afternoons
At Bagnigge Wells with china
  and gilt spoons
[Colman's prologue to Garrick's *Bon Ton*, 1775]

but by the 19th century the spa had declined into a resort of the lower classes, and in 1841 it closed. Tradition has it (on no very good evidence) that Bagnigge House was a summer retreat of Nell Gwynne, where she threw wild parties, and entertained Charles II with 'little concerts and breakfasts'. Although the house once boasted a bust of Nell, supposedly by Sir Peter Lely, it could well have simply been placed there by Hughes as an attraction. We nevertheless have Gwynne Place, on the Islington side of the road, spanned by the upper storeys of the

18  *Gardens at Bagnigge Wells, 1798.*

modern London Ryan Hotel. It leads to the nameless ascent to Granville Square immortalised in Arnold Bennett's *Riceyman's Steps* (1924), a novel which vividly portrays the district, aptly likening King's Cross Road to a 'canyon'. A second petrol station marks the location of the

Bagnigge Wells Tavern, built on the site of the spa's entertainment centre, licensed as a theatre from 1848 to 1874, and closed in the early years of WW II.

The hotel ahead stands on what were once Cold Bath Fields. Early houses built here were swept away to make way for

Rowton House, one of several London hostels founded by Lord Rowton to provide cheap, basic accommodation for working-class men. Opened in 1894 with 678 beds, it eventually closed in 1960, reopening the following year as the Mount Pleasant Hotel. The massive red-brick **Holiday Inn** now covers the site, serving an altogether better-heeled class of transients. Much water has flowed under erstwhile Black Mary's Bridge since Rocque's map of 1746 identified the hamlet here as Black Mary's Hole.

Immediately beyond the petrol station, turn right along the southern spur of Cubitt Street. The modern play centre at **No.3** extends onto the site of Model Buildings, an alleyway with very small cottages designed by Henry Roberts in 1844-5 for the Society for Improving the Condition of the Working Classes. The cramped environment was much criticised even at the time, and the embarrassed Society disposed of the property after only 10 years. By 1889 the street was another patch of 'very poor' blue on Booth's map.

A left turn leads into **PAKENHAM STREET**, on whose east side is an original terrace of 2-storey houses, with an unusually wide band of unrelieved brickwork above the first floor windows. Opposite the southern end of the terrace is an old industrial building, with barred windows on the ground floor, which has served at various times as a depot of the

London Improved Cab Co., as a dairy and bookbindery, and now as part of Camden Council's **Wren Workshops** (strictly, No.21 Wren Street). Following the street southwards, we are aware that although proceeding downstream, close to the old river bank, we are walking *up*hill! This is because the eastern end of Calthorpe Street (ahead) was built on artificially raised ground to avoid the kind of switchback observable further south at Mount Pleasant.

Pause at the **Pakenham Arms** on the corner of Calthorpe Street. Opposite is **PHOENIX PLACE**, dropping towards the natural level of the valley floor, here forming the modern Camden-Islington boundary, which has swung westwards following a meander in the course of the river. Another of the Fleet's several names was Turnmill Brook, and its banks hereabouts were once a hive of light industry. 19th-century Phoenix Place was home to colonies of wood turners and glass cutters, to the barrel-organ works of Pasquale & Co., and to the Phoenix Brass Foundry which stood at its southern end until seriously damaged in WW II. Just one building remains on the west side; otherwise, all is desolation. To the east, and now wholly in Islington, is the huge Mount Pleasant sorting depot of the Royal Mail. Opened in 1889 as the Parcel Post Office, it occupies the site of the notoriously harsh Cold Bath Fields Prison, or Middlesex House of Correction (1794-1877).

**CALTHORPE STREET**, an extension of Guilford Street, was developed in three stages. At the eastern end (which was built last), to the left of the corner on which you are standing, Camden Council's School House Workshops at **No.51** occupy a mid-19th-century building, originally a school of the (nonconformist) British & Foreign Schools Society. It later served, before WW I, as a drill hall of the Royal Army Medical Corps (Volunteers). The eye-catching bicycle shop at **No.50**, with its rusticated quoins, has a disappointingly mundane past, having served for half a century as a tobacconist's.

The central section of the street consists of half-stuccoed 3-storey houses of 1842-49. Follow it west to reach the unstuccoed 4-storey terraces at the earliest built west end of the street (1821-26), where **No.20** bears a blue plaque recording the residence in 1880-91 of the architect William Lethaby, a founder member of the Art Workers' Guild (p 26). Nathaniel Stallwood, the wealthy developer of this end of the street, lived at **No.21** on the corner of Gough Street. From his large balcony, now demolished, on the Gough Street frontage he witnessed the so-called Clerkenwell Riot of Monday 13 May 1833. A meeting of the unemployed, in support of working-class suffrage, took place in Cold Bath Fields. Banned by the authorities, it was brutally dispersed by contingents of the newly formed police. As the ensuing affray spread into surrounding

streets, PC Culley was stabbed on the pavement in Calthorpe Street, staggered to the yard of the Calthorpe Arms in Gray's Inn Road, and died. This is often said to have been the first ever killing of a constable on duty. The coroner's inquest became a *cause célèbre* when a jury sympathetic to the rioters returned a verdict of justifiable homicide, since the police had baton-charged the crowd without first reading the Riot Act.

Diagonally opposite No.21, **No.26** was the home in 1862-1911 of George Hare, an early maker of photographic equipment. It was previously occupied by Joseph Wright, co-founder of Wright & Horne, London's largest coach-building business, which in 1835 won the contract to supply most of the first-class mail coaches to the Royal Mail. The factory (c.1812) adjoining his house extended from **GOUGH STREET** to the river bank, and made omnibuses as well as coaches until it closed in 1852. The vacated space served later as stables, and was known as Royal Mail Yard; now it is mainly parking space. The backs of ultramodern office blocks in the Gray's Inn Road line the opposite side of the incongruously cobbled street.

Follow it southwards as far as **COLEY STREET** where, just short of the old St Pancras-Holborn boundary, we turn right to emerge again into **GRAY'S INN ROAD**. This was part of an ancient route to the north from the City markets, known originally as Portpoole Lane, but by Tudor times as Gray's Inn Lane. In 1660 General Monck marched 5800 troops along it to billets in Holborn, with the aim of restoring the monarchy; and in Fielding's *Tom Jones* the eponymous hero enters London by the same route. By the 18th century the east side had been built up as far as where you stand, while development at the northern (King's Cross) end began in the 1760s. The intervening stretch was built up in the first half of the next century, along with the estates bordering it on either side. Gray's Inn Road has often been described as 'dreary', with no real sense of purpose, and for this its unplanned, piecemeal development must be partly to blame. In 1862 the Lane became a Road, and the separately numbered terraces lining it were integrated within a single numbering scheme. The roadway was doubled in width by the Metropolitan Board of Works in 1879-80, and a decade later the London Streetcar Co. laid a tramway on it to run from King's Cross to a terminus at Holborn Hall.

The Coley Street corner is bounded by modern blocks, each recalling the thoroughfare's long association with the news media. To the south at **No.200** is the glassy 1986 headquarters of Independent Television News, its atrium descending into the basement area which once housed the giant presses of former Kemsley House, pre-WW II printing works of Allied Newspapers. Turn north past **Nos.222-236**, a long, mellower, arcaded block designed by Richard Seifert & Partners, built by McAlpine in 1974 for the Times newspaper group. Then named New Printing House Square, after the Thunderer's traditional City base, it housed *The Times* and *Sunday Times* until their departure for Wapping in 1986.

The building covers the site of St Bartholomew's, a very plain church of 1811, built as Providence Chapel for a coalheaver and preacher called William Huntingdon, SS (for 'Sinner Saved'). It became a Proprietary Episcopal Church a year later, and a District Church in 1860. 80 years later it was virtually destroyed by a bomb. North of the chapel once stood Leader's Coach & City Cavalry Stables, built in Old Merchant's Field, Gough's southernmost meadow, but swept away in the building of Calthorpe Street. The bizarre single-storey bed shop at **No.238a**, a modern creation, occupies the original site of the Central London Ophthalmic Hospital from 1843 until its move to Judd Street (p 71). The **Blue Lion**, on the west side of Gray's Inn Road, was relocated from the east side when its site was needed for the building of Wren Street. The earlier tavern had been nicknamed the 'Blue Cat' in mockery of its ill-painted sign.

Continue northwards as far as the **Calthorpe Arms**, which dates from c.1826, and retains its wood-framed windows. Turn right into **WREN STREET**, built progressively from 1824 to 1849, and called Wells Street until 1937 (since it approached the former spa). On the south side most of the original houses remain, 3-storeyed at the earlier western end with attractive ironwork, reducing to 2 storeys further east. At a bend in the road, the line of the frontage is preserved by an unusual free-standing stuccoed wall, pierced by two rounded arches serving as entrances to **Nos.15-16**. Opposite is **LANGTON CLOSE**, named after the Arthur Langton Nurses' Home on the west side (related to the adjacent former Royal Free Hospital), which was refurbished in 1995 as a hostel for students of University College.

North of Wren Street are pleasant **St Andrew's Gardens**, through the south end of which we now pass. The land here was acquired in 1747 as an overspill burial ground for St Andrew's, Holborn. Here were reburied the bones of the teenage poet Thomas Chatterton, and those of paupers from the Shoe Lane workhouse. Like the nearby St George's Gardens (p 51), the site was laid out as a public park in 1885 by the St Pancras Vestry; here, as in St George's Gardens, is a drinking fountain donated by Mrs Orbell. Leave the

*19   St David's Day, 1845. Boys processing from the Welsh Charity School, Gray's Road, sporting leeks in their military-style caps.*

gardens at the south-west corner in order to return to **GRAY'S INN ROAD,** and turn north.

At **Nos.141-153,** on the opposite (west) side of the road, are a few surviving houses in what was originally Foundling Terrace, where at No.2½ organ builder Henry ('Father') Willis opened his first shop in 1848-50. Pink-stuccoed **No.155,** spanning the entrance to a one-time signmaker's yard, is occupied by Barnes & Mullins, makers and subsequently wholesalers of musical instruments. Although a sign records the firm's establishment in 1895, the company moved to this site only c.1970, from Rathbone Place in Fitzrovia.

The neighbouring **Canolfan Llundain Cymry** (London Welsh Centre) houses an association (see also p 45) dedicated to the promotion of the Welsh language. Dating from before WW II, it was home during the conflict to the Welsh Services Club. Almost opposite, north of the old graveyard, once stood the Welsh Charity School, founded in 1718 for the 'education and welfare of poor children of Welsh parents born in or near London' (Fig 19, p 61). The school moved here from Clerkenwell Green in 1772, departing 85 years later for Ashford (Middx) where, as St David's School, it still exists. The Gray's Inn Road site was later occupied by Eley's ammunition factory; part of it subsequently reverted to more humanitarian use as a British Legion poppy warehouse.

**Trinity Court**, a 9-storey block of flats in concrete, with angular balconies, was built in 1935. It stands on the site of Holy Trinity Church, a Grecian-style edifice, erected in 1837 by James Pennethorne, with seats for 1,500 souls, and catacombs beneath for 1,000 bodies. It was restored in 1880, but closed in 1928, when the parish merged with that of St George the Martyr. In c.1872 a school was erected south of the church, built on arches to avoid disturbance to the graveyard. With the opening of the Prospect Terrace schools (p 81) in 1882 it became redundant. Its unremarkable building survives (as offices) at **No.252**.

Back on the west side of the road, at **No.167,** are the flats of **Jubilee House,** opened in 1985 to celebrate the 50th anniversary of the National Federation of Housing Associations, whose headquarters are next door at **No.171.** To the north, opposite a row of old houses once known as Mecklenburgh Terrace and now fronted by a modern showroom, is a granite horse trough erected in 1885 by the Metropolitan Drinking Fountain & Cattle Trough Association, inscribed with two apposite biblical texts, and some cryptic initials, presumably those of people related to the donor, a Mr E G Wood.

On the east side of the road (here originally Calthorpe Place) is the extensive site once occupied by the Royal Free Hospital. The first building here was the barracks built in 1812 for the Light Horse Volunteers, consisting of four blocks around a square courtyard. From 1830, they housed the factory of Thomas and George Seddon, cabinet makers and upholsterers. In 1843 the Free Hospital, by now under royal patronage, moved from Hatton Garden into the old barracks, ideally suited to the purpose of providing more beds. The northern Sussex Wing was added in 1856, followed by the Victoria Wing (1878) to the rear and, in 1895, the Alexandra Building, a splendid neoclassical block fronting Gray's Inn Road, its pediment adorned by the royal arms. In 1877 the Royal Free was the first hospital to admit female medical students; in 1895 it appointed the first Lady Almoner; and in 1921 opened England's first obstetrics and gynaecology unit. In 1926-30 the **Eastman Dental Hospital** was constructed on the charity school site to the south, designed by Burnet, Tait & Lorne, and sponsored by the American George Eastman, of Eastman-Kodak fame. After the removal of the Royal Free to Hampstead in c.1974, the main block served as offices of the Area Health Authority; the dental hospital has now expanded to fill the whole complex, in company with London University's Institute of Dental Surgery.

So we have come full circle. Buses running north and south stop nearby.

# South-east of King'sCross

With **KING'S CROSS** mainline station behind you, imagine the scene here three centuries ago when this was all open country. An old road ran north from Holborn along the lines of modern Gray's Inn and Pancras Roads; and a short distance in front of where you stand it crossed the Fleet river over a single brick arch called Battle Bridge. 'Battle' is probably a corruption of Bradford (or Broad Ford), perhaps how the river was crossed in earlier times. Tales that this was the site of a battle between Boudicca and the Romans, or between Alfred and the Danes, are wholly unfounded.

Local developers in the early 19th century wanted the area renamed to improve its image, long tarnished by the presence of Smith's dust heap at the top end of Gray's Inn Road (p 69) and the Smallpox Hospital on the King's Cross Station site. Early suggestions included Boadicea's Cross, Pancras Cross and St George's Cross. In 1830 Stephen Geary, architect of the Panarmonion (p 79), proposed that a monument be built, with a police station for the newly-formed force

in its base and above it a statue, to be paid for by public subscription, of George IV, the crossing to be renamed King's Cross. The suggestion was adopted, but the monarch inconveniently died, and by 1835 only enough money had been raised for a third-rate statue, hastily sculpted *in situ* from builder's composition while it dried (Fig 20). The police had meanwhile moved into the statueless base in 1831; when they outgrew their cramped station and left, it became a beer-shop. Continually mocked and satirized, and ill-lit at night, the 40ft-high monument was declared a public nuisance in 1845, and summarily demolished by the Vestry. However, King's Cross remained the name of the junction, and of the surrounding area, into whose south-eastern reaches we now venture.

Until c.1835 the acute angle between Gray's Inn and Pentonville Roads was occupied by a rustic tavern called the White Hart. A grander replacement, in more urban style and surmounted by a squat tower, was short-lived. In c.1860 the whole peninsular site was cleared for the construction of the underground Metropolitan Railway, to be refilled in 1873-4 by the 4-storey Italianate block

*20   The King's Cross monument to George IV. Saints George and Patrick (left and right) are balanced by David and Andrew, out of sight, on opposite corners.*

popularly known as the **'Lighthouse Building'**. Above the corner is a peculiar metal-clad wooden structure resembling a lighthouse, which until 1978 was largely obscured by advertising hoardings. Their removal prompted many ingenious theories as to the origins and purpose of the tower which, despite the best endeavours of local historians, remain a mystery. All that can be said with virtual certainty is that the tower served no practical purpose, but was rather a folly or architectural conceit intended to emphasise the importance of this junction of seven major roads, or maybe to enhance the marketability of a building erected directly over the railway tunnels, and thus much prone to noise and vibration.

Following the pavement to the left of the 'lighthouse', walk along the south side of **PENTONVILLE ROAD**, the first 200 yards of whose which are in Camden. **KING'S CROSS BRIDGE** (on the right) was constructed in 1910-12 to enable trams to run from the Caledonian Road without having to negotiate a very sharp curve at the 'lighthouse' corner. Although tramways were excluded from most of Central London, horse-drawn cars of the London Street Tramway Co. did penetrate down both King's Cross and Gray's Inn Roads from 1889, to terminate at Farringdon or Holborn. The tramway was taken over by the LCC in 1906 and electrified in 1911-12. King's Cross Bridge spanned the tracks of the Metropolitan

Railway, the world's first underground line, opened between Paddington and Farringdon in 1863 and initially served by steam locomotives. The original street-level buildings of the Metropolitan's King's

---

### Street names along route 8 and their origin

**Acton**
Acton Meadow, the field acquired by the Swinton brothers (earlier, Dry John's Field; Cottrell's Close)

**Britannia**
A patriotic name

**Field**
Battle Bridge Field

**Gray's Inn**
The Inn of Court at Holborn

**King's Cross**
A 19th-century monument to George IV stood at the junction

**Leeke**
Unknown

**Pentonville**
Islington suburb developed (1773-) by Henry Penton, MP

**St Chad's**
St Chad's Well, an 18th-century watering-place

**Swinton**
James and Peter bought part of the Calthorpe estate for building

**Wicklow**
Unknown

---

Cross station faced Gray's Inn Road, but they were demolished and replaced by a new station entrance on the west side of the bridge. Although the structure still stands, this entrance closed in 1941, when new platforms were opened beneath Euston Road, the original station having been destroyed in an air raid the year before.

Above the east side of King's Cross Bridge is the cupola of a former cinema, built in concrete on girders over the railway. The stuccoed baroque edifice, designed by H Courtenay Constantine, was started in 1914 but completed only after WW I, during which it was used to make aeroplane components. Opened in 1920 as the King's Cross Cinema, it later became the Gaumont, then the Odeon, closing under that name in 1975. In 1980 it played host to the Primatrium, an audio-visual ecological experience, before revival in 1982 as the Scala Cineclub, which in turn closed in 1993. The building is now shared by a nightclub and a pool club. Beyond the bridge, in Pentonville Road, is the glass-fronted **Thameslink** station, which opened in 1983 as 'King's Cross Midland City', and occupying part of the site of the original Met. station. Trains use the so-called 'Widened Lines', an extra pair of tracks built in 1868 to allow Midland and Great Northern trains to reach the City, and South London via Blackfriars. Beyond the station, the **Crossbar** nightclub was, until 1995, the

Bell public house, a classically styled early gin palace often attributed to the architect Stephen Geary (p 79), who ironically became a staunch supporter of the Temperance movement.

Veer right into **KING'S CROSS ROAD**. For much of its length the western (Camden) side is lined by mid-19th-century 3-storey houses, most with shops or places of refreshment on the ground floor, interspersed with 20th-century replacements such as **Instrument House**, named after its first occupants, Research & Control Instruments Ltd. In the frontage beyond, once known as Field Place, some attractive shop fronts survive, such as those at **No.205**, where the barber's 'Saloon' has a splendid gold-lettered fascia; and at **Nos.193-5**, premises of Dodd's the Printers, a firm long-established on this site.

Backtracking briefly, turn through an archway between Nos.195 and 197 leading into **ST CHAD'S PLACE**. This narrow eastern end, originally called Fifteen Foot Lane, leads through to the site of St Chad's Well, reputedly a medieval holy well, named for the patron saint of medicinal springs. By the late 18th century, it was a flourishing spa, 1000 people a week taking the waters here in 1772, when an annual subscription cost £1. By early in the next century it had declined into a weekend pleasure garden for locals, and despite attempts to revitalise it, eg by building a theatre for equestrian

events in 1829, the spa was soon to close. Houses were built on the west side, while the rest of the gardens were lost in the 1860s to the railway, which here follows the river valley southward in a cutting before tunnelling under a flank of Clerkenwell Hill. The building with an engaging lion's head above its doorway is all that remains of a Victorian tenement block called Stanley House, hence the sign on its side wall. This was the only site on this walk to be coloured deep blue (for very poor) on Booth's poverty map.

Turning left into **WICKLOW STREET** beyond the railway bridge, we penetrate the area which was once the eastern half of Battle Bridge Field. In 1767 a carpenter named Richard Hedges leased land here for house building. Other local tradesmen followed suit, creating a suburb of small Georgian houses, of which the street pattern is today the only reminder. Most of the estate had been demolished by 1900, either to make way for the railway or to be replaced later by assorted light industry and warehousing. Heavily damaged in WW II, the still cobbled streets are now almost deserted outside working hours, echoing only to the voice of the Thameslink train announcer. The northern end of Wicklow Street was known as Paradise Street until integrated with the southern part (George Street) in 1886.

On the left we pass a short stump (unlabelled) of **FIELD STREET**, which

was a through route to King's Cross Road before the removal of its railway bridge, its far end visible beyond the cutting. The street had its moment of fame as the spot where the getaway car was abandoned in *The Ladykillers*, Ealing Studios' black comedy of 1955.

Turn left along **LEEKE STREET**, passing on the corner an old industrial building now partly occupied by **Smithy's** wine bar. In horse bus days (c.1900) it housed stables of the London General Omnibus Company; 20 years later the rival bus company of Thomas Tilling was in occupation, doubtless motorised by then, but sharing the address with an independent farrier. Taking-in doors at the Wicklow Street end of the L-shaped block were possibly associated with the building's later use as a chromium plating works. Halfway down Leeke Street is the 1953 printing works of Vail & Co., a family firm founded locally by John Athy Vail in 1832. Beyond the railway **Nos.5-13** on our right, now an IT centre, have a grimy façade but a dignified pedimented doorway, inscribed '1890' and surmounted by a three-dimensional heraldic device: a gauntleted forearm with a sword hilt. It is perhaps no coincidence that a similar device serves as the crest of several families named Foster, and that the first occupiers of the building were Foster's Parcel Express Co.

On regaining King's Cross Road, observe on the far pavement a series of black metal posts inscribed 'SPPM' (St Pancras Parish Mark). Old photographs show identical posts lining the entire length of the road to mark the old limits of St Pancras and St James, Clerkenwell. Turn right, then right again into **BRITANNIA STREET**, the main thoroughfare of the early development in Battle Bridge Field. The patriotically named street was for many years flanked by George Street (George III), now the southern arm of Wicklow Street, and Charlotte Street (now Leeke Street). The **Golden Lion** pub, licensed as a theatre from 1854-64, was originally called the Golden Lions, and maybe the beasts involved were the heraldic ones of the royal arms. Between Britannia and Wicklow Streets is **Derby Lodge** (once Derby Buildings), a 'model' working-class tenement block in yellow stock brick, built in 1867-8 by the Improved Industrial Dwellings Company, and latterly managed by Camden Council. Its outside stairwells and landings reflect a Victorian preoccupation with through ventilation. Notice the diagonally patterned ironwork, repeated in Cobden Buildings, a companion block on the Islington side of King's Cross Road.

Walk as far as the crossroads with Wicklow Street. Opposite, at **No.27**, are the offices and conference centre of the National Association of Teachers in Higher and Further Education. Dating from 1900, the premises were for over 80 years

a bottled beer store of Whitbread's, hence the deer's head (the brewery's trademark) above the door. The Victorian building on the north-west corner was formerly St Jude's National School; the associated church (p 67) has long been demolished. The radical Unity Theatre first opened in the redundant school in 1936, moving a year later to its better-known home in Goldington Street.

Turn left down **WICKLOW STREET**, at the south-east end of which is a grey terrace of quite large surviving Victorian houses, dating from the period after the construction of the Metropolitan Railway. Turn right into **KING'S CROSS ROAD**, past the handsome **Northumberland Arms**, one of the road's earliest buildings, which had a theatre licence from before 1850 to 1874. Beyond a sharp southward bend in the road is **Finnegan's**, a tiny pub known as the Hansler Arms until 1997. On display inside is a manuscript mortgage deed of 1892, signed by Whitbread's and the landlord of the then recently renamed beershop. It was originally called the Noah's Ark, possibly a wry allusion to the regular flooding caused locally by a Fleet river very prone to bursting its banks.

Turn right, and up the south side of **SWINTON STREET**, built on land ('Acton Meadow') acquired from Henry Gough in 1776-8 by builder James Swinton and his brother Peter, a doctor. The street began as a short cul-de-sac off

Gray's Inn Lane, its eastern extension being completed only in 1844. Three-storey houses remain at the eastern end of the north side, most of which is now given over to the long, brick and glass, **Audiology Centre** of the late 1980s, and the **Nuffield Hearing & Speech Centre**, some two decades older, both associated with the nearby specialist hospital (p 67). The site behind them once contained Huskisson's chemical works, whose fumes must have blighted Victorian Swinton Street, much as the traffic of the King's Cross one-way system does today. On the south side, perched above the railway cutting, is a Victorian factory at **No.27**, once the cab-building works of the London Improved Cab Co. (*see also* p 58), and now, as the '**Atelier**', a collection of 14 workshops. An old terrace further west includes the **King's Head** pub, and **No.57**, which has a typical 18th-century black-painted wooden doorcase with a broken pediment.

Halfway along the street, turn south into **SWINTON PLACE**, a short roadway leading to **ACTON STREET**, where we pause. Like its northerly neighbour, Acton Street began as a short cul-de-sac, to be extended eastward between 1830 and 1849. Most of the original 3-storey houses survive, but **Nos.44-62** have been recently rebuilt. The **Prince Albert** pub on the north-east corner (to your left) is an ugly 1922 rebuild unworthy of a deviation, and a poor companion to the **Queen's Head** (a young Victoria), near the opposite end. Interestingly, this pub and the King's Head in Swinton Street are identical in size and stand exactly back-to-back.

Walk west to the junction with **GRAY'S INN ROAD**, and glance south to where a few early (c.1777) houses survive in what was once Constitution Row. Turn right (northward), however, past a series of unremarkable modern blocks, including **Headland House**, whose name recalls the earlier occupation of the site by the farmworkers' union. The Swinton Street junction is bounded by modern **Acorn House** (National Union of Journalists) and **Swinton House** (c.1930), whose occupiers include the Iron & Steel Trades Confederation, previously long established at No.78 Swinton Street. The doorway on the corner, still inscribed 'Bank', belonged to a long-closed branch of the National Provincial.

The **Water Rats** public house at **No.328** Gray's Inn Road refers to its present owners, the Grand Order of Water Rats (the entertainers' charity). Its theatre, noted in the 1970s as old-time music hall, still offers a variety of evening entertainment. Until c.1990 the pub

*21  The old Pindar of Wakefield tavern, drawn in 1724, a year after its destruction by a 'hurricane'.*

proudly bore the historic name of the *Pindar of Wakefield* (for the origin of the name, see p 79). That venerable tavern, patronised at different times by both Marx and Lenin, originally stood (Fig 21) on the opposite side of the road and south of Cromer Street (p 84), but was relocated here, the present building dating from 1878. Next door is the **Royal Throat, Nose & Ear Hospital**, opened 4 years earlier, with just ten beds, as the *Central London* Throat, Nose & Ear Hospital, a new wing being added in 1906. Sharing the site is London University's **Institute of Laryngology & Otology**, founded only in 1944, though the hospital had first

accepted postgraduate students some 80 years before. Immediately beyond, once stood St Jude's Church of 1862, designed by Joseph Peacock in a 'rogue Gothic' style, and built in red and yellow brick. It closed in 1936, its parish uniting with that of Holy Cross (p 84); Gray's Inn Road, which once contained three churches, then had none. No explanation has been found for the unexpected Continental-style shutters at **Nos.334-336**, which is now offices of the neighbouring Institute, and was previously a commercial laundry.

North of Britannia Street is a site once occupied by the large premises of the Home & Colonial Schools Society, an

Anglican institution founded in 1836 for the training of schoolmistresses. The pedagogical equivalent of a teaching hospital, it comprised four distinct 'model' schools, whose pupils paid upwards of 3d a week for the privilege of being 'practised' upon. By 1912 the establishment had moved to Wood Green, and was replaced by red-brick Pioneer House (c.1930). This, for some 30 years, housed various departments of the London Co-operative Society, including the Co-operative Press, along with the headquarters of *Reynold's News*. Part of it is now occupied by offices of the Open University at **Nos.344-352**.

Meanwhile, on the other (west) side of Gray's Inn Road, some houses dating from c.1824 survive. South of King's Cross, Gray's Inn Lane bisected an expanse known as Battle Bridge Field, owned in 1710 by the De Beauvoirs of Hackney. Its eastern half, which we explored earlier, had already been built on by 1800. The rest had been divided up and sold to a number of different owners, including Messrs Robinson, Dunston and Flanders, who in 1824 sought an Act of Parliament to authorise building. Houses in Chichester Place, as the west side of Gray's Inn Road was known here, were among the first to be built.

Easily missed is the unremarkable, but Grade II listed, arch at **No.277**. This was once the 'City Entrance' of the North London Horse & Carriage Repository (c.1827-8), an impressive classical structure (Fig 22) built around a courtyard, with a lavishly appointed assembly room at one end and a mansion at the other. North London's answer to Tattersall's, it offered high-class stabling and auction facilities, but apparently failed in this role, for the owner William Bromley had within 2 years transformed it into his Royal London Bazaar. In 1831 Robert Owen (Fig 23, and p 75) helped establish here an Institution of the Society to Remove the Cause of Poverty & Ignorance. The following year he opened his Equitable Labour Exchange, a short-lived co-operative enabling poor artisans to barter their skills for goods, using a

*22   The North London Horse & Carriage Repository, c.1828.*

*23 Robert Owen, painted in 1809.*

and guillotined French revolutionaries, was the forerunner of the Chamber of Horrors. After two seasons here Marie moved on to Baker Street, and the building was used for a furniture depository and then as a draughtsmen's office. As the 'Palace of Hygiene' it dispensed quack remedies; while as 'St George's Hall' the *piano nobile* played host to evangelists, panoramas and promenade concerts. In 1872 Whitbread's acquired the property, rebuilding it as a bottled beer store, which it remained until 1968. An elaborate Ionic portico, two storeys high, which had graced the Bazaar entrance was removed by the brewery to improve access.

Back on the east side, **Willing House** (c.1910) is an exuberant Tudor-Baroque assemblage designed by Hart & Waterhouse for the prosperous Willing's advertising agency. A statue of Mercury stands atop a pyramidal roof, winged lions support a large oriel window, while adorning the arched entrance are symbols of the advertiser's role as communicator. Removed to Mayfair c.1970, Willing's had been established locally since Victorian times, operating as 'showcard makers' at modest **No.366**, which still stands next door.

From here you may just glimpse (across King's Cross Bridge) a large painted legend on the exposed end wall of **No.370**. From 1873 until c.1910 this was the hall of the non-sectarian London Cabmen's Mission, which initially incorporated a cabbies' shelter. *THANKFULLY RECEIVED WITHIN*, says the sign, no longer specifying what is requested, though it was probably money!

Another painted sign remains visible on the façade of **Nos.319-321** opposite, recalling the presence here before WW II of Messrs Herbert & Co., makers of 'scales, weights and weighing machines'. Gray's Inn Road now bends quite sharply to the west so that, in ancient times, it could cross the river at Battle Bridge to follow the east bank northward along the line of Pancras Road. As you approach King's Cross, the grim frontage on your left fringes a site once occupied by an enormous, century-old, heap of dust and ashes, owned by one John Smith. There must have been organic refuse too, for the tip was said to provide forage for 100 pigs. The mound was finally removed only in 1826, when its contents were said (improbably) to have been sold to the Tsar to make bricks for the rebuilding of Moscow. With the heap removed, development of the western part of Battle Bridge field could proceed, but any hopes there may have been of raising the tone of the neighbourhood were thwarted by the presence of the Smallpox Hospital, and the later advent of the two mainline termini. We shall see efforts to do so (eg the aborted Panarmonion, and then Argyle Square, p 79) on Route 10, which also starts from King's Cross.

currency based on the value of labour. Sharing the premises was the Rev. Edward Irving, who came here with much of his congregation after his expulsion from Regent Square (p 82). Neither stayed long: Irving disliked being associated with Owen, who himself soon moved on (ejected, some say) after a dispute over rent. In 1833-5 Mme Marie Tussaud settled here with her waxworks after 26 years of touring. A 'Second Room, inadvisable for ladies to visit', featuring death masks of murderers

# Route 9
# The Skinners' Estate & Euston Road

Leaving King's Cross Underground station by the exit from the Metropolitan Line on the south side of Euston Road, follow the signs for Camden Town Hall, and walk along the south side of Euston Road to where the Town Hall's old and new halves are separated by a narrow footway, once the northern end of Tonbridge Street. Turn left into it, and then right along **BIDBOROUGH STREET**. Bidborough is a village near Tonbridge (Kent), and the two names are an indication that we are entering the Skinners' estate, on which we shall see several Kentish locations featuring in the street names. In 1572 Sir Andrew Judd vested the land in the Skinners' Company as trustees for the school he had founded at Tonbridge in response to the dissolution of the monasteries. Known as Sandhills (or Sandfield), the property extended westwards to Burton Street, as well as north-eastward onto the site of the future St Pancras station. From c.1807 building leases were granted to James Burton, who had already developed a large part of the Foundling estate to the south.

At the east end of Bidborough Street is the **Dolphin** pub, one of several sites of which the livery company still owns the freehold. The **Camden Centre**, formerly St Pancras Assembly Rooms, and part of the Town Hall block, faces the north side of **Queen Alexandra Mansions**, one of many blocks of red-brick mansion flats

---

### Some street names along route 9 and their origin

**Bidborough**
A village near Tonbridge (qv)
**Burton**
James, speculative builder of much of the area
**Cartwright**
Major John (1740-1824), the 'Father of Reform'
**Duke**
The 4th Duke of Bedford (fl.1756)
**Euston**
Suffolk seat of the Duke of Grafton
**Flaxman**
John (1755-1826), sculptor
**Judd**
Sir Andrew (fl.1572), founder and benefactor of Tonbridge School
**Leigh**
Place near Tonbridge
**Mabledon**
Place near Tonbridge
**Tonbridge**
The Skinners' Estate endows Tonbridge School

---

built round here before WW I by the London Housing Society (LHS), a limited company that was still based in Judd Street till about 1978. A blue plaque recalls the residence here in 1914-36 of the war artist Paul Nash. A neighbour of his in 1916 was the actress Mary Clare, leading lady in Noel Coward's *Cavalcade*.

Avoiding the singularly charmless west end of the street, turn left into **JUDD STREET**. Built in the early 19th century as a continuation of Hunter Street, its west side here is occupied by more LHS mansion flats and the **Skinners' Arms** pub, predating 1839. This is another Skinners' freehold. Opposite, at **No.123**, and once known as Kelvin House, is an unlabelled British Telecom building dating from just before WW II, which served as the North Trunk (later International) Exchange. To its south is the Social Services Headquarters of the **Salvation Army**, opened by General William Booth in 1911, formerly home to a uniform and bonnet factory, and now accommodating the archives and permanent exhibition of the Army's International Heritage Centre. **Nos.85-103** form a stuccoed terrace of houses (possibly by Burton), some with old shop fronts, including the fine Corinthian specimen at **No.95**, a former butcher's. Back on the west side of Judd Street are **Medway Court** flats, where a north-facing plaque celebrates the completion here in 1955 of the 2000th dwelling built by St

Pancras Council since WW II. A Camden branch library occupied a unit on the ground floor until St Pancras Library opened at No.100 Euston Road in 1971.

South of Leigh Street, **Nos.62-63** are two Burton 4-storey houses of 1808-11. The cherubic statuette above the doorway at **No.63** has no obvious significance. Now a patisserie, the premises were for generations a sweet-shop. Beyond, a service ramp descends into what was once Hunter Place, long home to the local police station. The building over the ramp fronting on Judd Street began as replacement headquarters for No.8 Police District. Later, as McNaghten House, it was a council-run hostel for the homeless. Now named the 'Generator', and with an entrance in Compton Place (p 51), it is part of a private-sector international chain of hostels for more privileged young travellers.

Beyond, on the corner of Tavistock Place, the 'luxury studios' now dubbed **Albany House** were once the Central London Ophthalmic Hospital, which moved here from Gray's Inn Road (p 60) in 1913. When it closed in 1948 it was converted to house the University's Institute of Ophthalmology (now sited next to Moorfields Hospital). Opposite is **Clare Court**, 1920s flats behind grand gilded railings supporting coats of arms and the fatalistic motto *Quod Deus vult*, a last outpost of borderline Bloomsbury before

it melts into vulgarian King's Cross.

Backtrack slightly up Judd Street. North of Clare Court is an open space known to bureaucrats as **Judd Street Gardens**, but to everyone else as Bramber Green, from the name of an adjacent block of flats. Saved from office development, it opened in 1954 on a plot of ground which had been a temporary home to the ever-moving King's Cross Coach Station. Notice the images of plane-tree leaves cut into the tops of the boundary railings.

Turn right along **CROMER STREET** (also p 84), whose western end lay on the Skinners' estate. On the corner is the **Tonbridge School Club**, founded in 1882 jointly by the Kentish school and the Judd Foundation. It originally combined the functions of boys' club and mission hall, but the two functions were split when Holy Cross Church (p 84) was opened. The present building, dating from 1932 (as a stone recalls) is now shared by a youth club for both sexes and the more prominently labelled College of Karate.

Just to the east is the early-19th-century incarnation of the **Boot** tavern. Before 1800 it was, as the Golden Boot, one of the few buildings in the area. As well as liquor it offered a tea room and skittle alley, while adjoining it to the north and west were Bowling Green House and its two greens. Bowls was then often an excuse for the kind of rowdy behaviour for which this early leisure complex was

infamous. In *Barnaby Rudge*, Dickens portrays the Boot as the headquarters of his fictional band of troublemakers in the 1780 Gordon Riots. Adjoining the pub is **Speedy Place**, a short (once longer) alley leading nowhere, its name commemorating a family whose tenure as landlords of the Boot spanned three centuries.

The roadway in front of the tavern once contained an ice house, and was known as Greenland Place; nine houses had been built here as early as 1741. **Bramber** flats cover the site of No.5, Thomas Bryson's piano works; and of No.4 (later No.123 Cromer Street), known fancifully as 'Nell Gwynne's Cottage' and as 'Compo Castle' because of its elaborate composition mouldings placed there by an early owner, nicknamed 'Compo Jack' — possibly the builder James Lucas. Set back from the street, surmounted by a lion *passant*, and adorned with Hebrew inscriptions and grotesque heads, it served various commercial purposes until 1938, when it was wantonly destroyed, demolished as part of an Air Raid Precautions exercise. The German bombs which fell nearby would probably have spared it!

Turn left into **TONBRIDGE STREET**, the eastern boundary of the Skinners' estate, where no original houses remain. At the south end are **Tonbridge Houses**, a model dwellings block of 1904 built by the East End Dwellings Company (also p 85), whose sphere of operation extended outside the area suggested by its name. Peace Cottages, which previously stood on this site, were doubtless euphemistically (or apotropaically) named. Further north, on the east side, is **Argyle Primary School**, opened by the London School Board in 1880 but misleadingly inscribed '1902', the date of its enlargement.

Turn left again into **HASTINGS STREET**, which as Speldhurst Street, was briefly home to the widowed Mary Shelley and her small son Percy soon after their return from Italy in 1823. Once again, LHS mansion flats dominate the scene, and nothing survives of the houses built by Burton and his contemporaries. Recrossing Judd Street, turn left along **THANET STREET**, where on the east side **Nos.8-17** are a delightful row of half-stuccoed 2-storey workers' cottages, probably by Burton. The west side is lined by two more LHS blocks, between which is the modern **International Lutheran Students' Centre**, on the site of the National School of 1872 (Fig 24) by William Milford Teulon, younger brother of Samuel Sanders Teulon. After the start of WW II the school was named Thanet Hall and put to various commercial uses until it was demolished in 1976. At the end of Thanet Street, turn left into

*24  W M Teulon's Thanet Street National School (from The Builder, 6 April 1872).*

**LEIGH STREET**, built in 1810-13 by Burton and others. Henry Mayhew, founder of *Punch* and author of *London Labour & the London Poor*, lived at its western end in 1850. On the largely intact south side, some attractive old shop fronts remain, along with a mixture of small shops and eating places which has long characterised the street. The front doors of some houses are approached by several steps, the ground floors raised to allow as much light as possible into very narrow basement areas. On the opposite site, the tiled Victorian **Norfolk Arms** once had a smaller companion two doors away on the Thanet Street corner, the 'Suffolk Arms'; but it was a beer retailer's rather than a pub.

Walk north along **SANDWICH STREET**, where a range of 4-storey houses similar to those in Leigh Street remains at **Nos.1-9**. The street was long a centre of services to the poor: a soup kitchen in 1848 was followed by a parochial library, and in 1873 by neo-Gothic St Pancras Mission Hall, designed by W M Teulon, with a school adjoining at the rear. After WW II, the hall was let, and later sold, to the Lutherans. **St Mary's German Lutheran Church** was founded off the Strand in 1694 as the church of St Mary-le-Savoy. Its c.1976 rebuild, here on the mission hall site, is below ground, with a student hostel above.

Turn left along Hastings Street, and pause to look north along **MABLEDON PLACE**, where the sole surviving house at **No.12** was once the Sandhills estate office. The rebuilt pub now called **Mabel's** was the Kentish Arms until 1968, when it became the Escape, displaying memorabilia of WW II prisoners of war. **No.1**, the tall concrete tower of UNISON, the major public service trade union, was built c.1976 for NALGO, one of its constituent parts. Mabledon Place was widened in 1902, at the same time losing a protective bar gate at the north end. In 1850 this corner hit the headlines, when a stag, pursued from Hendon by the huntsmen and hounds of one Mr Bean, negotiated the streets of Somers Town, crossed the New Road and, terrified by the traffic (even then!), leapt over the Mabledon Place bar (Fig 25, p 74) to seek sanctuary in an ironmonger's shop.

On the east side of the Place is **Hamilton House** (1913), headquarters of the National Union of Teachers. On this site, at No.19, the poet Shelley stayed on business in 1817, visited alternately by wife Mary, then seeking a publisher for her *Frankenstein*, and his stepsister-in-law Claire Clairmont. To its north is **Bidborough House**, an undistinguished 1960s office block containing Camden Housing Department. Here once stood the factory of Messrs Voile & Wortley, listed in 1859 as dry-salters, but a century later as makers of liquorice. The site had been occupied in 1818-30 by a riding school, and later by livery stables. A statue of a horse which once graced Voile's premises now stands in the inner courtyard of the modern block.

South of Mabledon Place is **CARTWRIGHT GARDENS**, built by James Burton in 1809-20, and known as Burton Crescent until 1908. In Trollope's *The Small House at Allington*, John Eames takes lodgings there, falling prey to the wiles of the landlady's daughter Amelia. Porticoed **No.26**, at the north end, was home in the 19th century to the St Pancras Royal General Dispensary; and after 1911 to a pioneering day nursery, which later evolved into the Caldecott Community. Walk south along the crescent's north-south diameter, which was damaged in WW II and is now lined on the left, eastern side by **Hughes Parry**, **Canterbury** (with winged cherubs) and **Commonwealth Halls**, three London University halls of residence built progressively over two decades, on a long lease from the Skinners.

**Commonwealth Hall** bears a brown plaque commemorating the residence in 1837-9 at erstwhile No.2 of Rowland Hill, the former teacher whose 1837 pamphlet on Post-Office Reform led to the establishment of the Penny Post two years later. Hill's neighbour at No.1 was the social and public-health reformer Edwin Chadwick; novelist John Galt lived at No.9 in 1813-14; No.10 was home in 1841-44

74

to church architect Edward Buckton Lamb; and No.18 is thought to have been a London pied-à-terre of William Moon, remembered for his system of embossed print for the blind. Nos.20 & **34** were successive homes in 1835-9 of the peripatetic Sydney Smith. In 1908 the crescent was re-named after another former resident, John Cartwright, a former naval man, later a major in the Territorial Army, who lived at **No.37** from 1820 until his death 4 years later. Known as the 'Father of Reform', he campaigned for manhood suffrage and against slavery. A bronze statue in his honour, unveiled in 1831, sits in the central gardens, now given over to tennis courts for use by residents.

The crescent's change of name may have been prompted by the stigma attached to it by two horrible murders, including the unsolved 'Burton Crescent Murder' of 1878, when Rachel Samuel, an elderly widow, was battered to death at No.4. A female former servant of hers was charged with the offence, but was acquitted for lack of evidence. *The Cartwright Gardens Murder* (1924), a long-forgotten detective novel by J S Fletcher, concerns a wholly unrelated fictitious case of poisoning, set here in what it described as a 'drab and dismal crescent'.

*25   Mabledon Place bar, 12 Feb 1850: Mr Bean's stag hunt comes to town.*

Burton's western circumference survives intact, though much altered. The south-west curve, up which we turn, surprisingly appeared on Booth's poverty map in deep blue (for very poor), reflecting the presence there at **No.45** of the Society for the Rescue of Young Women & Children, and at **No.49** of the Main Memorial Home for Deserted Mothers. **Nos.51-53** were a YMCA hostel in 1920, but since before WW II this quadrant has been occupied by small hotels, which are not always decorated in the best of taste. View from here the north-west curve, which is lined by **Cartwright University Halls** (formerly Bentham Hall), including **Nos.31-33**, home in WW II to the Club for Educated Women Workers, later the Club for Students & Professional Women.

Turn left along short **BURTON PLACE**, originally Crescent Place, where Robert Owen lived in the 1830s at No.4, a house adjoining, at the rear, a major hub of his many activities (see below). On the south side today is **Virginia Court,** a 1994 pastiche which has, like **No.5** opposite, an imposing portico modelled on a surviving original at the opposite end of the Place. Behind is **Woolf Mews**, a contemporary development in what was once South Crescent Mews. (The Woolfs, incidentally, lived not here, but in Tavistock Square, a little to the west.)

**BURTON STREET** was developed in 1809-20 by the eponymous builder.

Though under threat of demolition in 1973, the houses at the south end have been spared and restored, preserving the attractive (if mass-produced) trelliswork of their individual balconies. Most have 4 storeys, and would have been classified as 'first-rate' had they not been so narrow. **Nos.14-16** rise to only two storeys, possibly because the money ran out. Burton often sublet leases to other builders, and breaks in brickwork here point to the houses' separate construction. At the far south end of the street once stood No.17, a substantial villa in its own grounds, which was home in the 1830s to John Britton, cellarman turned topographer and antiquary, and later housed the Burton House Collegiate School (previously in Regent Square). Latterly occupied by an ugly British Rail garage, the site is now covered by the sympathetically-styled housing association flats of **Leonard Court** (c.1994).

Burton Street was once a cul-de-sac at both ends, which explains its curious numbering scheme, starting in the middle opposite Burton Place, and running anticlockwise along the SW, E and NW sides to where it began. There was once a gate here giving access to old Tavistock House, which Burton had built as his own home. The rear of the present Tavistock House (Lutyens' replacement, headquarters of the BMA) lines the north-west side of Burton Street, and now houses the bookshop of the British Medical Journal. Watercolourist George Sidney Shepherd died at No.47 in 1858. The ubiquitous Rev. Sydney Smith lived on the site in 1839-44 at No.54, near to a synagogue at No.51.

A rainbow of faiths made use of the Burton Street Hall (demolished 1927), whose site is marked by the modern infill on the opposite side at **No.39**. Built for the Particular Baptists in 1811, it was later used by the reformer Robert Owen (p 68). The London Co-operative Society held its inaugural meeting here in 1824, before installing itself in Red Lion Square, and Owen continued to use the hall for his 'social festivals' (or lectures) until 1837. Thereafter it was used by the Swedenborgians and, from 1849, as the St Pancras Free Church, which was not a nonconformist establishment but an offshoot of the nearby parish church, providing 275 free seats for the poor. Later still the hall became St Mary's RC school, then a Salvation Army citadel.

The roadway linking Burton Street with Duke's Road (to the north) did not exist before 1906. A flight of steps led down into what had been Draper's Place, described in 1860 as a vile slum where 'squalor, disease and death were rampant with immorality and crime', and where typhus and gaol fever were rife. Renamed Brantome Place in 1885, it was swept away, along with adjacent North Crescent Mews, for the

building by St Pancras Council of **FLAXMAN TERRACE** (1907-8). Designed by Joseph & Smithern, red-brick **Flaxman Court** is topped by two copper cupolas, exuding the civic pride of the day. Set repeatedly in the railings, barely discernible through successive layers of paint, is the Council's badge depicting the boy martyr Pancratius. Opposite is an annexe of The Place (see below), housing the Contemporary Dance Trust, and standing on the site of the Victorian piano factory of Eavestaff & Sons. **Flaxman House** is an unusually grand caretakers' lodge, with its own pair of cupolas, and now occupied by an architectural practice.

**DUKE'S ROAD**, along which we continue north, dates from the 1760s. It stood on the boundary of the Fitzroys' Tottenhall estate, hence the name of **Grafton Mansions** (1890) on the east side, Duke of Grafton being one of the family's several titles. However, the road takes its name from another peer, the 4th Duke of Bedford, who vigorously opposed the building of the New Road but eventually realised its benefits and upgraded a trackway running north out of his Bloomsbury estate to serve as his own private road to it. **Nos.2-10** on the west side are a fine terrace of former shops, an extension at right angles of Woburn Walk, Thomas Cubitt's delightful shopping parade of 1822. They are now stuccoed and used mainly as offices, their smart

black shop-fronts redundant. **No.22**, on the south-east corner, now offices, was until the early 1930s the butterscotch factory of Messrs Callard & Bowser.

The edifice we know as **The Place** was opened by the Prince and Princess of Wales in 1889 as the drill hall of what was later named The Artists' Rifles, TA. Its early volunteers included Millais, Holman Hunt, William Morris, and Robert Edis, the building's architect. Its site was earlier occupied, from 1846, by the Lord Nelson Music Hall, also known as the Euston Music Hall, the New Music Hall and Frampton's. The drill hall is now home to a dance school, and the Place Theatre is London's foremost modern dance venue.

For weary walkers, nearby Euston station now provides an escape route. Otherwise, cross **EUSTON ROAD** and walk east towards King's Cross along its north side, for a better view of the south side which concerns us here. South Row, the stretch of the New Road east of Duke's Road, was first developed in the 1790s in a corner of Lord Somers' estate, and was thus, strictly, part of Somers Town. The 1756 Act of Parliament which authorised the construction of the New Road stipulated that no new buildings be erected within 50 feet of the carriageway, so as not to impede troop movements. The terraces of large houses which at first lined the road therefore had long front gardens. In the 19th century many of the gardens

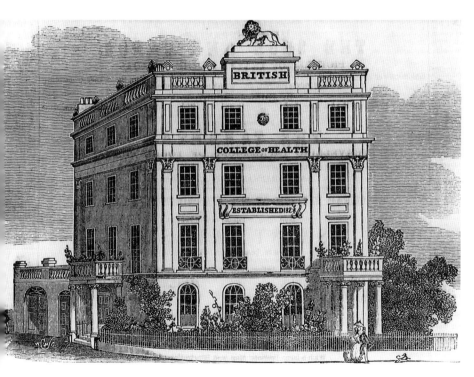

*26 The 'British College of Health', on the site of the present Camden Town Hall Extension.*

were acquired by monumental masons, who filled them with their statuary. Here in South Row was a colony of funerary specialists, including a mason's, a marble works, and factories making coffins, wreaths and crosses. Penetrating this small industrial enclave was Inwood Place, named after the locally based family of architects. Blitzed in WW II, the site is covered by a 1960s block of offices and council flats, now the **Travel Inn** hotel, currently (1998) decorated in a virulent blue. The name Somerton House has been retained. This recalls Somer*set* Terrace, a former tributary of Duke's Road, where suffragette Emmeline Pethick(-Lawrence) shared lodgings with her friend Mary Neal, the morris-dancing revivalist.

Beyond Mabledon Place, in what was once Tonbridge Place, the red-brick offices of 1930s **Clifton House** and the **Euston Flyer** pub (1998) cover a site earlier used briefly for a 'Euston Market'. The gloomy 1950s railway offices of Great Northern House have been cheerfully refurbished as the **St Pancras International Youth Hostel** (No.79). This stands on the site of the Euston Cinema, damaged beyond repair in WW II, which was in turn built on the site of the Congregational Tonbridge Chapel (founded 1810); a century later it served as the Christian Catholic Church in Zion, an American evangelistic establishment.

At the junction with Judd Street is the

erstwhile Euston Tavern. Rebuilt after wartime damage, it became **O'Neill's** Irish theme pub in 1996. **Camden** (formerly St Pancras) **Town Hall** was opened in 1937, replacing the Vestry Hall near Old St Pancras Church. Steel-framed, faced in Portland stone, and roofed in Westmorland slate, it was dismissed by Pevsner as 'unremarkable neo-Palladian'. The site was Hamilton Place in the early 19th century; the architect E B Lamb lived here in 1828-9. Later, the houses were colonised by offices of coal merchants and colliery agents, whose trade flourished in the railway lands to the north. They were demolished in the mid-1920s, after which the vacant site was used temporarily for a small funfair, complete with 'figure of eight' rollercoaster.

The 8-storey **Town Hall Extension**, designed by the Council's own architects, sprouted on the Argyle Street corner in 1977-8. **St Pancras Library** moved into the ground floor in 1993, on vacating its 22-year-old purpose-built home at No.100 Euston Road. The unloved, unlovely modern block stands on the site of a much-loved theatre, opened at Nos.37-43 in 1900 as the Euston Palace of Varieties. Here Marie Lloyd performed, and actress Kay Hammond made her 1927 debut in *Tilly of Bloomsbury*, a romantic comedy by Ian Hay. Successively renamed Euston Theatre, Euston Music Hall, and Regent Theatre, it became a cinema in 1932, later renamed the Century, then the ABC, before closing as the Granada in 1968, to end its days as a bingo hall. No.33, on the corner site, was occupied until WW II by a Red Shield hostel of the Salvation Army, earlier by a temperance hotel, and before WW I by the pretentiously named British College of Health (Fig 26, p 77). This was actually the research and manufacturing base of the firm founded by James Morison (d.1840), creator of the world-famous Morison Vegetable Pill. A genuine medical establishment, the British Hospital for Diseases of the Skin, existed in 1906 at No.29, where Barclay's Bank now stands on the corner of Belgrove Street.

Back at King's Cross, stand in front of the mainline station and look over to the south side of Euston Road, where the amusement arcade at **No.1** was, from 1897 until the 1960s, the elegant Reggiori's restaurant, a Swiss-Italian establishment much admired for the stained glass of its 'cathedral' windows. Notice how the original houses here were set back from the road to respect the 50-foot rule (p 76), and how their gardens were later covered by single-storey shops.

## Route 10
# South of King's Cross

Emerging from King's Cross Underground station on the south side of Euston Road, walk a few yards eastward to the top of **CRESTFIELD STREET**, begun, as Chesterfield Street, in 1825, even before the removal of Mr Smith's tip (p 69). It was one of several short streets named until 1937 after prominent peers of the realm or their seats, and built by W Forrester Bray on the site of the New Road nursery garden. On the east side is the plain brick post-WW II incarnation of **King's Cross Methodist Church** (p 86). Now return along Euston Road and turn left along **BELGROVE STREET**, another of Bray's creations, the west side lined by some of the small private hotels which have characterised the Battle Bridge estate since the late 19th century. These former houses (Bray originals) were praised by the LCC's *Survey of London* for their 'admirable execution' and 'ingenuity of design'. In stark contrast, the east side is wholly dominated by the ugly brick premises behind 1930s **Belgrove House**. Home at first to the King's Cross Coach Station, they might have become a cinema, but instead served later as a GPO garage and sorting office, now closed.

Continue south along either side of **ARGYLE SQUARE**, built after 1832 on part of the site of the projected Royal London Panarmonion. This grandiose scheme was to have occupied all of the area now contained by Argyle, Birkenhead and St Chad's Streets. Probably the brainchild of Gesualdo Lanza, an Italian music teacher, it was meant to include a music academy, a large theatre flanked by ballroom and refreshment rooms, a gallery and hotel, reading and billiard rooms, and a botanical bazaar, all set in pleasure gardens, with the added attraction of a 'suspension railway', which was a sort of monorail, with a person-powered boat-shaped carriage (Fig 27, p 80). The architect was Stephen Geary (p 65), better known for his design of Highgate Cemetery. The project was a complete flop, and its promoters faced bankruptcy. Although the gardens were laid out, it is uncertain whether any of the buildings were even started, but what little might have been built was demolished in 1832, to be replaced by houses with characteristic round-arched doorways and ground-floor windows, some partly stuccoed.

On Booth's poverty map the square appears as a splash of middle-class red, and census returns confirm a high proportion of artists and professionals. Walter Crane, chiefly remembered as a children's book illustrator, but then aged 17 and an engraver's apprentice, was living with his widowed mother at **No.46** in 1862. By 1900 the square was largely given over to private hotels, as it still is, their garish modern signs often jarring with the restrained 19th-century architecture. The east and west sides are almost intact, but the south-east corner was destroyed in WW II, taking with it the New Jerusalem Church (replaced by Sandfield flats, p 85). Built for the Swedenborgians in 1844, it was neo-Norman style, in white and yellow brick, with twin 70-ft spires. Unassuming **No.30** nearby on the south side was once the Salvation Army's Prison Gate House, a hostel for discharged prisoners.

Forming part of the south side of the square is L-shaped **ARGYLE STREET**, along which we turn left. Its east-west section was begun, as Manchester Street, in 1826, but not completed for another 14 years. (For the north-south section see p 85.) Organ builder Henry Willis had one of his numerous workshops at No.18 (on the Gatesden flats site) in the 1850s.

At **GRAY'S INN ROAD** turn right (south), passing the 19th-century **Lucas Arms** at the end of Cromer (once Lucas) Street and, beyond at **Nos.235-243**, the site of the ancient Pindar of Wakefield tavern. This was named not after the ancient Greek poet but after a legendary Yorkshire folk hero, a contemporary of Robin Hood, and a bane of King John's tax collectors. A pinder was one responsible for penfolding or impounding

# SUSPENSION RAIL-WAY, ROYAL PANARMONION GARDENS,

## LIVERPOOL STREET, KING'S CROSS, NEW ROAD, St. PANCRAS.

## WILLIAM THE FOURTH, ROYAL CAR.

This astonishing Machine, now exhibiting in the Royal Panarmonion Gardens, is perhaps one of the most simple pieces of Machinery ever discovered, possessing such wonderful action, that many tons weight may be conveyed to any distance, without the help of steam or animal power. No one can believe that this Car travels with such ease and rapidity without being a witness of the fact. The idea is a very ingenious one, and does great credit to Mr. H. THORRINGTON who is the inventor. The admittance to the Gardens is One Shilling each Person, entitling the parties to ride round the gardens in the Car, or on the Hobby Horse. Refreshments may be obtained on the Premises.

stray cattle. Recorded in 1575 as being the only hostelry between Holborn and Highgate, it was destroyed by a 'hurricane' in 1723, and the landlord's two daughters were buried in the rubble. It was subsequently rebuilt on the east side of the road at No.328 (p 67). **No.233**, an unmarked brick building of the late 1930s, once served as TERminus telephone exchange, and the metal frames of its huge windows are adorned by flaming torches and a series of stylised early handsets enclosed in wreaths.

Turn right into **HARRISON STREET**, built in the southern part of a meadow called Peperfield, acquired in 1783 by Thomas Harrison, described as a farmer, though his family had by then already been brickmaking for 160 years. The development of the Foundling estate to the south persuaded them that more money could be made from houses than from bricks. Nothing remains of the old street, where Paul Storr, gold- and silversmith to the royal family, working to designs by Flaxman, opened workshops at No.17 in 1819. Post-WW II blocks of council housing now line most of both sides of the street. The rebuilt **Harrison Arms** stands on the corner of **SEAFORD STREET**, a short, now wholly 20th-century street,

*27  The monorail at the ill-fated Royal Panarmonion may have been erected and tested, but probably never carried passengers.*

which we follow southward. Modern flats here include **St Peter's Court**, sole reminder of the Greek Revival church in Regent Square, whose site they occupy. Others replaced small factories, including a toy factory, chromium and nickel plating works, and Walmsley's button factory, which survived WW II to become makers of board-game components.

**SIDMOUTH STREET**, connecting Gray's Inn Road to Regent Square, was built by the Harrisons in 1807-18, though it had been planned as early as 1799. To the east, on the north side today is the post-WW II Sidmouth Mews development of low-rise council-flat blocks which have, perversely, Sussex place-names (because they lie in the 'Sussex' zone of St Pancras Council's block-naming masterplan). On the south side, erstwhile No.25 was the family home in 1840-43 of James William Hudson, a pioneer of adult education. By coincidence, its site is now covered by the Gray's Inn Road site of **Kingsway College**, latter-day providers of such enlightenment. Opened in 1958, the building initially housed the LCC's Starcross Upper School, a good mile south-east of its parent establishment near Euston station. The site was previously occupied by the Prospect Terrace Board Schools (1882) and public baths, devastated in wartime bombing. These in turn had supplanted Georgian Wellington Square, with its Prince Regent tavern,

and the slums of diminutive Derry Street. Diagonally bisecting the site, 'Prospect Terrace' had long been the main entrance driveway to the twin burial grounds which became St George's Gardens (p 51). Sidmouth Street's only remaining houses, at **Nos.51-55**, have unusually narrow first-floor windows. "Bates's salve cures wounds and sores" boasts an old painted inscription on the end wall of **No.55**, the base before WW II of Messrs Bates & Co., makers of magnesium citrate.

When the first houses appeared in Gravel Pit Field in 1829, George IV had become king, but **REGENT SQUARE** had been planned and named by the Harrisons years before, under the Regency. The first buildings were the two elegant churches in contrasting styles which were to be the square's glory until WW II. On the east side was Anglican St Peter's (Fig 28, p 82), designed by William Inwood and his son Henry, the architects of St Pancras New Church in a similar Greek Revival style, with a two-stage tower and a hexastyle Ionic porch. Begun in 1822, it was consecrated 4 years later and flourished until WW II, when it suffered a direct hit. The portico survived till 1967, when despite vigorous protests it suffered a fate similar to that of Euston Arch.

In the south-west corner of the square was a Presbyterian chapel, whose congregation moved here from Hatton Garden. Known as the National Scotch

(or Caledonian) Church, it was designed by Sir William Tite in a decorated gothic style (Fig 29), intended as a miniature version of York Minster. Thomas Carlyle was at the stone-laying in 1828, and Coleridge and Robert Peel were at the opening 3 years later. The congregation adhered to the Church of Scotland until the Disruption of 1843, when it joined the English Presbyterians. Its most famous minister in 1822-32 was the Rev. Edward Irving (Fig 30, p 84), whose unorthodox style of worship, which encouraged 'speaking in tongues', led to his expulsion by the church authorities for heresy. He and 800 of his followers subsequently took refuge at the Royal London Bazaar (p 68). Damaged 'beyond repair' in a V2 attack in 1944, the chapel was demolished and replaced by the plain brick **Regent Square United Reformed Church**, incorporating the national headquarters of the URC.

A terrace of old houses survives on the south side of the square, where **No.6** was home for some 17 years to artist William Coldstream, a co-founder with Victor Pasmore (p 22) of the Euston Road School. **Nos.4-6** from c.1863-1904 were

*28  St Peter's Church (Regent Square) in 1828, consecrated 2 years earlier, but still set amidst the Harrison brickfields (from the Gentlemen's Magazine).*

the Homes of Hope, for young women deemed too good for the workhouse because of their previous good character; by 1919 they had become a base of the Women's Training Corps. Isaac Seabrook, the builder of both the Inwood churches, lived at **No.1** and No.27 1832-1844. Council flats line three sides of the once war-ravaged square. On the north side (at No.36) lived James Strachey, brother of Lytton, and translator of Freud's writings, listed by Vanessa Bell as an original member of the Bloomsbury Group, an association he always denied. On the west side, No.18 was home in 1848-50 to Angier March Perkins, the celebrated American-born steam engineer. Aldous Huxley lived briefly in 1921 at No.26 while his wife and baby were abroad, Huxley having recently become a journalist for *House and Garden*. The gardens of Regent Square, noted for their lofty plane trees, gained notoriety in 1917 when the dismembered body of a woman was found there wrapped in brown paper. Louis Voisin, a Belgian butcher, had murdered an ex-lover at a house in Fitzrovia, and made use of his vocational skills to dispose of the corpse.

Leaving the square in the north-west

*29 York Minster in miniature: the Scotch Church, Regent Square (1829 etching, after a painting by T H Shepherd).*

corner, follow a footway northward past **Glynde Reach** flats, to **CROMER STREET**, once the most notoriously rough street in the area. Originally called Lucas Street, it became so disreputable that by 1828 it had been renamed, after either the Norfolk fishing village or the peer of the same name. Running just north of an old track leading westward from Gray's Inn Lane to the Boot tavern (p71), the street was developed in 1801-15 by Joseph Lucas, a tin-man (or tinplate worker) of Long Acre, who had inherited 7 acres of cow pasture in the northern half of Peperfield. We emerge into the street alongside **Holy Cross Church**, financed partly through the generosity of the Goodenoughs (p 44), and dedicated in 1888. It replaced a mission hall opened 12 years earlier in what is now Argyle Walk. Towerless, and with a plain and undistinguished exterior somewhat redeemed at the time of writing by colourful murals on the west wall, it was designed by Joseph Peacock, also architect of neighbouring St Jude's (p 67), from which some fittings were brought when the parishes merged in 1936. The church was always regarded as High Anglican, and in 1996 one mass each week was celebrated by a Roman Catholic priest, some of the congregation having converted to the RC faith the previous year. Long noted for its charitable work, Holy Cross now houses in its crypt

a drop-in centre for vulnerable people.

After heavy damage in WW II, little survives of old Lucas Street, where William Fletcher, said to have been valet to Lord Byron, set up in business making drain-tiles, partnered by two Italian brothers called Lambelli, employing technology long used in the latter's homeland for the extrusion of macaroni. No trace remains of the Baptist chapel which existed here in 1839-68, of the later hall of the London City Mission, or of the LCC's Cromer Street School. Gone are the terraces of houses and shops which once lined the street, the Silver Cup pub (predating 1838) which failed to survive WW II, and the Marquis of Wellesley, which did not even make WW I. On the south side, set at right angles to the street, and separated by lawns is a series of balconied, brick-faced, 6-storey blocks of the late 1940s designed by Robert Hening and Anthony Chitty. Like their blocks for Holborn Council (p 18), these won the commendation of Pevsner, who liked their symmetrical arrangement. Their appearance has changed dramatically since 1995 in an imaginative refurbishment of the whole estate by Camden Council. The ends of two buildings are dignified by the (post-1936) coat of arms of St Pancras borough, the elephants being the giveaway.

Some blocks are named arbitrarily after places in Sussex, the county chosen by St Pancras Council postwar planners

*30   The charismatic Rev Edward Irving (1826 engraving).*

to inspire block names in this part of the borough; other names are of local historical interest. **Great Croft** was an earlier name for **Peperfield**, the field beneath our feet. The name might derive from 'peppergrass', an old word for 'cress', for the area was noted in the 18th century for the watercress which thrived beneath the elmwood pipes of the New River Company, which crossed 'Peperfield' on the surface, leaking profusely. **Hollisfield** was the area developed as Argyle Square; **Mulletsfield** recalls Thomas Mullett, proprietor in the 1790s of Bowling Green House (p 71); **Sandfield** has already been noted as the nearby Skinners' property. The Sandfield Centre, on the latter's ground floor, is home to the Bengali Residents' Association, reflecting the high proportion of Bangladeshis in the local community. **Bedefield** recalls the de Bedefields, 14th-century landowners in the Lay Manor of St Pancras, and **Gatesden** one John de Gatesden, lord of the manor in 1247.

Running north off Cromer Street are four short, narrow, sloping streets. Although most of this area, despite its reputation, appeared on Booth's poverty map in pale blue (for 'mixed'), these little tributaries were shown in black, denoting 'vicious, semi-criminal'. Here some houses were shared by five families, and many of the women scraped a living making artificial flowers. In Dutton (now

Tankerton) Street, a Mr Caslon was, in 1818, pioneering the manufacture of gas, which he delivered to customers in wire and canvas drums. A ragged school for boys moved here from Compton Place (p 51) in 1855. Slum clearance in the 1890s led to the erection by the East End Dwellings Co. (EEDC) of six 4-storey model dwelling blocks, with an experimental mixture of stairwell and balcony access, the balconies floored with expensive York stone. Four newer blocks were added along the Cromer Street frontage in the 1930s, one named after Edward Bond, first chairman of the EEDC. In 1987 Camden Council proposed demolition of four of the older blocks, replacing **Kellet House** with an open space to be known as Kellet Square. After an outcry by residents, the properties were instead sold to the Community Housing Trust, and in 1998 the **Hillview Estate**, as it is now known, was in the throes of a 5-year programme of rehabilitation, with much input from a caring and vocal residents' association. Some original square-cut wrought-iron balconies have controversially given way to modern 'Juliet'-style replacements. The profusion of window-boxes is not new: in 1892 the EEDC set aside £10 a year for prizes to encourage window gardening.

Enjoy a ramble around this unusual 19th-century survival, taking in **TANKERTON STREET**, **MIDHOPE**

**STREET** and **LOXHAM STREET**, where Loxham House is a 1948 rebuild. Linking their northern ends, and continuing west to Tonbridge Street, is the very Victorian footway called **ARGYLE WALK**. The EEDC had wanted to name it 'Cromarton Walk', while locals preferred their own nickname of 'Plum Pudding Steps'. The path's undulating progress is interrupted by the occasional shallow step: the original early 19th-century development was so cheapskate that nobody troubled to level the ground.

Follow the footway westward, and turn north down **WHIDBORNE STREET**, where **No.6**, the solitary old building at the north end, is a former butcher's. Alongside are the crumbling remains of Argyle School gates, with separate entrances for boys and for girls and infants. The school itself has turned its back on the street which gave it its name, and now faces Tonbridge Street (p 71). It was built on a triangular piece of land not wanted by the Panarmonion Company, let in 1832 to a Golders Green farmer, whose 'St Pancras Dairy' boasted a cowshed 300 feet long. **McGlynn's** at No.5 is yet another Irish 'theme pub', known until 1996 as the Duke of Wellington.

Started in 1832, the north-south section of **ARGYLE STREET** (*see also* p 79) has always been known by its present name. From outside the **Wardonia Hotel** look north towards the Midland Grand Hotel, and experience a scene screened repeatedly in *The Ladykillers* (also p 65). This was supposedly the view from Mrs Wilberforce's front door, though her house was actually a mock-up specially erected off Caledonian Road 1½ miles away! Little changed today, the scene is still dominated by small hotels converted from houses of the 1830s.

Continue north and turn right into **ST CHAD'S STREET**, originally called Derby Street, hence modern **Derbyshire House**, headquarters of the Central Council for Education and Training in Social Work. At the eastern end, beyond Argyle Square, a few old houses of 1827-8 survive as offices or hotels, technically 'third-rate' but with very ornate wrought iron balconies. The garage access opposite was once the 'Grand Entrance' of the Royal Bazaar (p 68), where another fine Ionic portico was demolished long ago by Whitbread's.

Intersecting from the north is **BIRKENHEAD STREET**, begun by Bray in 1825, and named Liverpool Street until 1938. Entry to its historical southern end is now barred by security gates, erected in 1996 as part of Camden's King's Cross Estate Action scheme. **Riverfleet** flats, within the fortress, mark roughly the site of the 'Royal Entrance' to the old Bazaar and the offices (at No.11 Liverpool Street) of the Panarmonion

Company. Turn north along the rump of Birkenhead Street, whose east side is lined by Bray houses, converted long ago into small hotels of the kind which traditionally provided workspace for prostitutes, earning King's Cross its perennial reputation as one of London's 'red light' districts. Here in Birkenhead Street in 1907 was the Female Preventive & Reformatory Institute & Midnight Meeting Movement; 'midnight patrols' were still being made by the Salvation Army in 1974 from a base at Faith House (No.11 Argyle Street); and in 1982 the English Collective of Prostitutes staged a lengthy occupation of Holy Cross Church (p 84), after eviction from premises nearby.

King's Cross Wesleyan Chapel opened on the west side of Liverpool Street in 1825, with W H Smith (later of bookstall fame) among the original trustees. It was enlarged in 1865-6, with a mission hall facing Crestfield Street (p 78). Rebuilding after WW II reversed the arrangement, with the church facing Crestfield Street, and the church hall, now **Methodist Chaplaincy House**, here in Birkenhead Street. **No.61**, to the north, marks the site of a little theatre opened in 1830 as part of the Panarmonion scheme, and the only element of it to be completed. It was meant to be used for tuition and rehearsals, but was pressed into revenue-earning service when the parent project collapsed. It survived, precariously, for

some 50 years, with several changes of ownership and eight changes of name, but is perhaps best remembered as the Royal Clarence or Cabinet Theatre. Polini and Edmund Kean were among the famous actors who trod its boards. The site was later absorbed into Reggiori's restaurant (p 78), the strikingly classical building picked out in blue and white which rounds the corner into Euston Road. 1997 saw the opening of a new '*Police Office*' on the opposite corner, occupying an old branch of the Capital & Counties Bank. Thus the Metropolitan Police has at last returned to King's Cross, over 150 years after deserting the base of the monument which once stood directly opposite, and which gave the district its name.

# Sources

## Books

Aston, Mark. *The cinemas of Camden* (Camden Leisure Services, 1997)

Barker, Felix & Silvester-Carr, Denise. *Crime & scandal: the black plaque guide to London* (Constable, 1985)

Barker, TC. *Three hundred years of Red Lion Square* (Camden Libraries, 1984)

Bebbington, Gillian. *London street names* (Batsford, 1972)

Booth, Charles. *Life and labour of the people in London (Macmillan, 1892-7).* 9 volumes and 1 volume of maps

British Printing Industries Federation. *11 Bedford Row* (The Federation, 1995)

Department of the Environment. *List of buildings of special architectural or historical interest as at 14 May 1974, London Borough of Camden* (DOE, 1974)

Fairfield, S. *The streets of London: a dictionary of the names and their origins* (Macmillan, 1983)

Godber, Joyce. *The Harpur Trust, 1552-1973* (The Trust, 1973)

Gordon, Edward & Deeson, AFL. *The book of Bloomsbury* (Edward Gordon Arts, 1950)

Green, Shirley. *Who owns London?* (Weidenfeld, 1986)

Hair, John. *Regent Square: 80 years of a London congregation* (Rev ed., James Nisbet, 1899)

Hamilton, Godfrey Heathcote. *Queen Square: its neighbourhood and its institutions* (Leonard Parsons, 1926)

Hunter, Michael & Thorne, Robert (eds). *Change at King's Cross, from 1800 to the present* (Historical Publications, 1990)

Lehmann, John. *Holborn: an historical portrait of a London borough* (Macmillan, 1970)

McClure, Ruth K. *Coram's children: the London Foundling Hospital in the eighteenth century* (Yale U.P., 1981)

McGee, John Edwin. *A crusade for humanity* (Watts, 1931) [on the Positivist School]

National Hospital. *Queen Square and the National Hospital 1860-1960* (Edward Arnold, 1960)

Nichols, R.H. & Wray, F.A. *The history of the Foundling Hospital* (Oxford U.P., 1935)

Pepper, Peter. *A place to remember, the history of London House* (Benn, 1972)

Pevsner, Nikolaus. *London, except the Cities of London and Westminster* (Penguin, 1952) (The buildings of England)

Summerson, John. *Georgian London.* New [4th] ed. (Barrie & Jenkins, 1988)

Survey of London, Vol.24: *King's Cross and neighbourhood* (London Survey Committee; LCC, 1952)

Tallis, J. *London street views 1838-40.*

Tames, Richard. *Bloomsbury past* (Historical Publications, 1993)

Weinreb, Ben & Hibbert, Christopher (eds). *The London encyclopedia* (Macmillan, 1983)

Whitley, W.T. *The Baptists of London, 1612-1928* (Kingsgate Press, 1928)

## Biographical

*The dictionary of national bibliography*

Hobhouse, Hermione. *Cubitt, master builder* (Macmillan, 1971)

Jerome, Jerome K. *My life and times* (Alan Sutton, 1984)

Leslie, Anita. *Madame Tussaud, waxworker extraordinary* (Hutchinson, 1978)

Sherry, Norman. *The life of Graham Greene, Vol.2* (Cape, 1994)

Sobel, Dava. *Longitude* (Fourth Estate, 1996)

Wilson, Jean Moorcroft. *Virginia Woolf, life and London: a biography of place* (Cecil Woolf, 1987)

*Who was who*

## Maps

Rocque, 1746

Booth's poverty maps, 1889-98

Goad's insurance maps

Bomb damage maps (at GLRO/LMA)

Ordnance Survey, 1866-71 (and later)

## Other sources

*The Antiquary*, April 1908 [on the *Horse Repository*]

*Camden History Review:* Mrs Humphry Ward vol 2 pp7-8; Rifle Volunteers vol 3, pp30-31; block names vol 8 pp27-28; model dwellings vol 9 pp4-9; Fleet river vol 11, pp10-14; no.4 Parton Street vol 13 pp15-18, *see also* vol 20 p8; New Road vol 15 pp15-19; Working Women's College vol 16 pp29-33; Panarmonion & King's Cross vol 17 pp13-16; mailcoach building vol 18 pp6-9; Cabmen's Mission vol 21 pp25-29

*Camden New Journal*

*Community News* (King's Cross & Brunswick Neighbourhood Association, 1980-86)

*St Pancras & Holborn Chronicle*

Census returns

LCC/GLC street lists

Post Office/Kelly's London directories

Ratebooks (St Pancras; and the United Parishes of St Andrew and St George the Martyr)

East End Dwellings Co. Minute books, 1891- (Tower Hamlets Local Studies Library, Bancroft Road, E1)

CINDEX, database of Camden Information Services (London Borough of Camden)

National Monuments Record, 55 Blandford Street, W1

Camden Local Studies & Archives Centre, 32-38 Theobalds Road, WC1 (including the Heal Collection)

Guildhall Library, Aldermanbury, EC2

London Metropolitan Archives, Northampton Rd, EC1

Westminster Archives, St Ann's Street, SW1

# Index

90

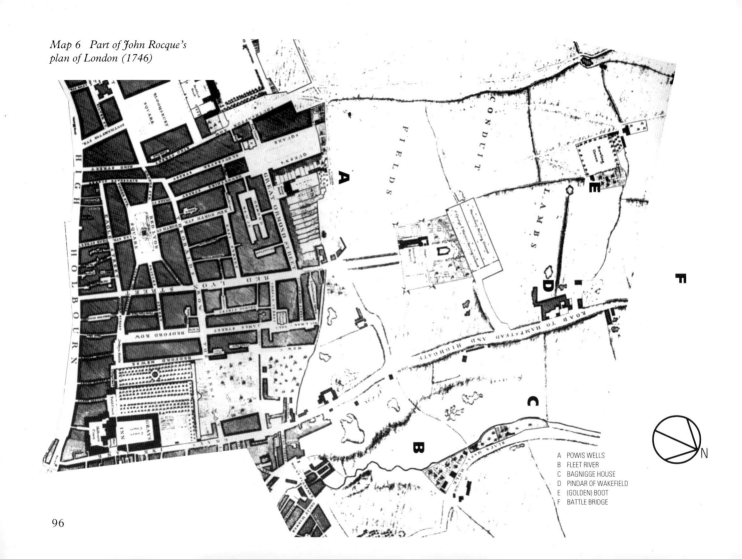

Map 6 Part of John Rocque's
plan of London (1746)

A POWIS WELLS
B FLEET RIVER
C BAGNIGGE HOUSE
D PINDAR OF WAKEFIELD
E (GOLDEN) BOOT
F BATTLE BRIDGE

96